Abounding Grace

Abounding Grace

The Book of 2 Corinthians

This inductive Bible study is designed for individual, small group, or classroom use. A leader's guide with full lesson plans and the answers to the Bible study questions is available from Regular Baptist Press. Order RBP1646 online at www.regularbaptistpress.org, e-mail orders@rbpstore.org, call toll free 1-800-727-4440, or contact your distributor.

REGULAR BAPTIST PRESS
1300 North Meacham Road
Schaumburg, Illinois 60173-4806

*The King James Version is the English translation used
in our Sunday School curriculum.*

The Doctrinal Basis of Our Curriculum
A more detailed statement with references is available upon request.

- The verbal, plenary inspiration of the Scriptures
- Only one true God
- The Trinity of the Godhead
- The Holy Spirit and His ministry
- The personality of Satan
- The Genesis account of creation
- Original sin and the fall of man
- The virgin birth of Christ
- Salvation through faith in the shed blood of Christ
- The bodily resurrection and priesthood of Christ
- Grace and the new birth
- Justification by faith
- Sanctification of the believer

- The security of the believer
- The church
- The ordinances of the local church: baptism by immersion and the Lord's Supper
- Biblical separation— ecclesiastical and personal
- Obedience to civil government
- The place of Israel
- The pretribulation rapture of the church
- The premillennial return of Christ
- The millennial reign of Christ
- Eternal glory in Heaven for the righteous
- Eternal torment in Hell for the wicked

ABOUNDING GRACE
Adult Bible Study Book
Vol. 54, No. 1
© 2005
Regular Baptist Press • Schaumburg, Illinois
www.regularbaptistpress.org • 1-800-727-4440
Printed in U.S.A.
All rights reserved
RBP1649 • 0-87227-413-6

Contents

Preface 7

Lesson 1 Comfort in Uncomfortable Trials 9

Lesson 2 Sincerely Yours 19

Lesson 3 Give Me Liberty! 29

Lesson 4 Hidden Treasure 37

Lesson 5 A Change of Address 47

Lesson 6 God's Diplomatic Corps 55

Lesson 7 Dare to Be Different 65

Lesson 8 Repentance Brings Relief 75

Lesson 9 Charity Begins in the Heart 85

Lesson 10 The Joy of Giving 93

Lesson 11 Apostle in the Crosshairs 103

Lesson 12 Bragging Rights 111

Lesson 13 Ready or Not, Here I Come 119

Preface

When you hear the word "grace," what comes to mind? A female friend? a famous sports star? a mealtime prayer? Perhaps you have learned the classic definition of "grace," "God's unmerited favor." Usually we associate God's unmerited favor with salvation.

But God's grace goes beyond salvation. It provides strength for ordinary, everyday living and for out-of-the-ordinary trials (2 Timothy 2:1). God's grace abounds: God supplies as much as you need, whenever you need it, as often as you need it. No matter what you are facing, God's grace can see you through.

So what are you facing today? Financial problems? failing health? a so-called thorn in the flesh? difficult children? backstabbing? unjust criticism? deep personal problems? misunderstandings? Paul faced more than his share of trials. In his second letter to the Corinthians, he testified to the power of God's grace to have victory over them; he also demonstrated God's grace in his attitude toward the troublesome Corinthian believers. And the good news is, God's grace is available to you today as much as it was to Paul.

As you study 2 Corinthians, use this study book for additional information and insight. Learn and meditate upon the key verses and thoughtfully answer the questions you find in each lesson. The more effort you put into your personal study of 2 Corinthians, the stronger you will grow in God's abounding grace.

Comfort in Uncomfortable Trials

2 Corinthians 1:1–11

"Blessed be God, even the Father of our Lord Jesus Christ, the Father of mercies, and the God of all comfort; who comforteth us in all our tribulation, that we may be able to comfort them which are in any trouble, by the comfort wherewith we ourselves are comforted of God" **(2 Corinthians 1:3, 4).**

Remarks like the following punctuate every prayer service in Bible-believing churches:

"Please pray for my husband. He has been experiencing a lot of pain after injuring his back."

"I'd like to request prayer for my mother. She is a strong Christian, but she is having a hard time coping with the report that she has liver cancer."

"Let's keep praying for Bart and Melinda. As you know, Bart lost his job recently, and Melinda's health has not been good."

"Pray for the Smiths in Bangladesh. They lost their house and possessions in the devastating flood that hit that country last week."

Do you wonder why God's people suffer? Have you recently encountered pain or trouble and asked, "Why me?" If these hard questions trouble you, peek over the shoulders of the first-century Corinthian believers and read the opening part of 2 Corinthians, the inspired letter that Paul wrote to them. It provides the answers we all need.

Getting Started

1. What kind of suffering do you think is the hardest to endure? Why?

2. What are some common things people turn to for help during suffering?

Searching the Scriptures

Paul wrote this letter to the church in Corinth. Many would have doubted that a church could survive in that big, bustling seaport. Corinth was located on an isthmus, a slender piece of land three and one-half miles wide that connected two large areas, northern and southern Greece. The isthmus lay between two gulfs. Ships would come to Corinth to be unloaded in one gulf; then the ships would be wheeled overland and reloaded in the other gulf. It was more economical to do this than to sail all the way around southern Greece. Since travelers from far and wide crossed through Corinth, a multitude of languages could be heard in that city.

Not surprisingly, Corinth was a pleasure-mad city. Part of that pleasure came from the Isthmian Games, which were headquartered there. Gladiators fought to the death as the citizens of Corinth cheered or jeered them. Life was held cheap in Corinth, as reflected in the nature of the Games and in the extensiveness of slavery. The slave population may have been as high as 75 percent.

How could a Christian church survive in Corinth? Sensual pleasure and self-indulgence characterized the city. For example, religious prostitution thrived. The temple of Aphrodite alone had a thousand prostitutes! The entire Roman Empire knew of Corinth's wickedness. The Romans even coined a saying, "to live like a Corinthian," to describe people with loose, immoral conduct.

The church in Corinth had its problems, as one might expect. Paul wrote to try to get the Corinthians to put the church in order. In that letter, which we call 1 Corinthians, he dealt with the problems of division, immorality, lawsuits between Christians, drunkenness and gluttony at the Communion table, and misuse of spiritual gifts.

We may piece together from 2 Corinthians 2:1 and 4, 12:14, and 13:1 and 2 that Paul had visited Corinth after writing 1 Corinthians. During that visit, he had confronted the church about its failure to resolve the issues he had discussed in 1 Corinthians. Later he wrote a second letter (a lost letter that God did not place in the New Testament), rebuking the Corinthians for their unwillingness to take remedial action. Finally he received word that the church had repented, so he wrote 2 Corinthians from Macedonia and followed it with a personal visit (Acts 20:1–4). However, a group in the Corinthian church still opposed Paul and scoffed at his claim to be an apostle.

3. Read 2 Corinthians 1:1. To what did Paul attribute his apostleship?

The will of God

It is amazing to think that some Corinthians still doubted Paul's apostleship after the suffering he was willing to endure on their behalf. Perhaps they did not like what they read in his first two letters to them. Undermining his authority would give them an excuse to ignore his rebuke and warnings.

4. How might the following designations from verse 1 have encouraged the Corinthians?

"the church of God" *The Corinthians believers would know they were Gods people*

"saints" *They would know they were separated unto Him.*

5. Grace and peace are gifts from God the Father and the Lord Jesus Christ (v. 2). Why do you value

grace? *Grace is the means where by God saves us*

peace? *is the result of being saved*

6. The word "blessed" means literally "speak a good word." What two reasons did Paul give in verse 3 for speaking a good word for God?

The reasons are Gods mercies (Kindness) and comfort

Paul intentionally emphasized God's blessedness. About to launch into a discussion on suffering, Paul wanted his readers to understand that all suffering must be seen against the backdrop of God's blessedness.

7. What is significant about God's being the God of *all* comfort?

Genuine lasting comfort comes from God nothing else

Drugs alchal hobbies etc

As the fountainhead of mercy and comfort, God is willing and able to sustain His children through suffering. We need not panic or pine (sigh) in our afflictions, because He "comforts us in all our tribulation."

8. How has a trial given you a deeper appreciation of God's comfort?

Trials teach us patient and strengthen our faith.

In verses 4–11 Paul presented **five reasons why God allows suffering.** *Comfort others*

9. According to verse 4, what is (one reason) why God allows believers to suffer?

God allows us to suffer so we might be able to comfort others with the comfort we experienced during our suffering.

Talking to someone who has been through a trial similar to the one you are experiencing can provide you with a huge lift.

10. What sufferings have you experienced that now provide an opportunity for you to minister to others?

11. Describe a time when someone who had experienced a trial helped you with a similar trial.

The **second reason** for suffering is so we will know and appreciate the comfort that comes from Christ.

12. Read 2 Corinthians 1:5. What is the correlation between suffering and Christ's comfort?

As our suffering gets worse God's comfort gets greater

Paul was well-acquainted with the comfort of Christ. Because of his devotion to the Savior, ungodly men opposed him, and intense trials dogged his steps. Nevertheless, the Savior's comfort abounded toward him (v. 5). Similarly, every affliction we encounter because we stand for Christ and serve Him brings with it an unlimited supply of divine help.

A **third reason** God brings us trials and suffering is found in verses 6 and 7.

13. Who did Paul say would benefit from his suffering (vv. 6, 7)?

The Corinthians

As God was comforting Paul in his trials, he was an example to the Corinthians. In essence, Paul's experiences benefited the Corinthians by his modeling how to respond to trials.

Beginning in verse 8, Paul told the Corinthians of an experience that took him to the depths of despair. It happened somewhere in Asia. Paul did not say precisely what happened to him. Perhaps he was referring to the time when Demetrius the silversmith opposed the preaching of the gospel and started a riot against him (Acts 19:23–40). But it does not seem that Paul was apprehended in the riot. So some suggest that a near fatal illness caused Paul to despair. And others have suggested that Paul was referring to shipwreck or persecution or to the problems heaped on him because of rebellion by the Corinthian church.

14. According to 2 Corinthians 1:8, how did Paul describe the degree to which he suffered? *It was beyond his ability to handle it / He thought he would die because of it*

15. Describe the role Paul's own strength played in helping him through the trouble he described (v. 9).

He didn't trust himself He knew it was beyond his ability to handle it

God was teaching Paul to rely on Him during trials. Reliance on God is the **fourth reason** God allows suffering in our lives.

The trouble Paul experienced was severe. He thought he had reached the end of his life and that death was knocking on the door. He wrote that he "despaired even of life" and "had the sentence of death" in him (vv. 8, 9).

16. What situation has taught you to rely completely on God?

Serie sickness with Kidney Sherie problems.

17. What would you say to a Christian who claims to be desperate?

Calm down and wait on the Lord.

Prayer and thanksgiving form the **final reason** God allows us to experience trials and suffering.

18. What evidence do you see that prayer works (vv. 9–11)?

Paul Knew the prayers of the church was the reason. He overcame his suffering

Paul was delivered out of his life-threatening crisis partly because the Corinthians prayed for him. He testified, "Ye also helping together by prayer for us." Because the Lord answered the Corinthians' prayers, many believers offered thanks (vv. 10, 11).

19. Has anyone ever thanked you for praying for him or her?

20. How did the Lord answer your prayers for that person?

21. According to the following passages, how should you pray for others?

Romans 1:9 *~~Without Thanks~~ . With out ceasing*

Ephesians 1:15, 16 *With Thanks*

2 Timothy 1:3 *With a pure conscience*

Making It Personal

22. Select one person who is undergoing a difficult trial.

___Allen Asay___

What specific action will you take this week to comfort that person?

Call Him. Send him a card. go by and see him.

23. a. List the three most prevalent trials you are now facing.

(1) *job*

(2) *my brothers*

(3) *health*

b. Meditate on the following Scripture passages. Ask God to supply you with His abounding grace so you might face your trials with peace and confidence.

Psalm 23:4

Psalm 71:19–21

Psalm 119:49–52, 76

John 14:27

Philippians 4:6, 7

1 Peter 5:7

24. Call a friend and ask him or her to pray for you in the midst of your trial.

25. Commit 2 Corinthians 1:3 and 4 to memory. Write the verses below.

Lesson 2

Sincerely Yours

2 Corinthians 1:12—2:17

"For we are not as many, which corrupt the word of God: but as of sincerity, but as of God, in the sight of God speak we in Christ" (2 Corinthians 2:17).

Shopping for a sports coat and tie, a gentleman tried on a plaid coat. However, it was too small to accommodate his expansive waist. Tight creases flanked the middle button that seemed ready to pop, and the sleeves ended two inches above his wrists.

"Looks like a perfect fit," commented the salesclerk. "And that purple tie you're holding should complement the ensemble."

Obviously the salesclerk was either insincere or blind.

Wouldn't you rather do business with a sincere salesperson than to receive false accolades from one who simply wants to make a sale?

Those who profess to serve the Lord must support their profession with sincere words and actions.

Getting Started

1. When have you observed insincerity?

2. Why do you value a pastor who speaks the truth in love?

Searching the Scriptures

False teachers who had infiltrated the Corinthian church accused Paul of serious shortcomings. They rejected his apostolic credentials and charged that he was insincere, fickle, and untrustworthy. Paul defended himself against their allegations. He was confident that his godly conduct among the Corinthians for eighteen months proved his accusers wrong (2 Corinthians 1:12).

3. What three aspects of his behavior among the Corinthians did Paul cite (v. 12)?

Paul had nothing to hide. Anyone willing to look honestly at the evidence of Paul's life had to conclude he was sincere. But his opponents did not stop there. They charged that Paul wrote deliberately obscure letters that often stated one thing but meant another.

4. What did Paul write concerning his letters (v. 13)?

No one had to read between the lines for hidden meanings in Paul's letters. Paul always wrote what he meant and meant what he wrote.

In verse 14 Paul mentioned the coming "day of the Lord Jesus." The day of the Lord refers to the day believers stand before the Lord their judge.

5. What is the focus of the day of the Lord (2 Corinthians 5:10)?

Paul knew the Corinthians would rejoice in his ministry to them and recognize it as sincere in the day of the Lord. Those Corinthians who refused to acknowledge Paul's sincerity did not discourage Paul. He realized that Jesus saw his heart, and he knew that Jesus saw sincerity.

Paul's attackers also claimed he was fickle, that he did not keep his promises. This accusation focused on Paul's announced intention to visit the Corinthians. He had informed them in a previous letter that he hoped to visit them twice, once on his way to Macedonia (northern Greece) and again on his way back. Thus they would receive a "second benefit" (2 Corinthians 1:15, 16), that is, they would be blessed by two visits from the apostle.

It was a good plan, but it did not work out. Something stopped Paul from going, and Paul's opponents seized the opportunity to attack him. They charged that he was unreliable and two-faced, saying one thing and doing another.

Paul informed the Corinthian believers that they could not call his trustworthiness into question (v. 17). He was, after all, their apostle.

6. Since Paul was the Corinthians' apostle, who did they implicate by doubting his trustworthiness (v. 18)?

God had chosen Paul and had entrusted him with the gospel. Because God is faithful, He does not commission double-tongued messengers who say, "Yes, yes," when they mean, "No, no."

7. How effective will a Christian's witness be at work if he or she consistently misses meetings and neglects e-mails?

Paul based the stability of his character on the stability of the Lord. Jesus Christ was not yes and no but a firm, positive yes (v. 19). Moreover, the promises of God are affirmative (v. 20). Christ is the fulfillment and fulfiller of all God's promises; He is their sum and substance.

8. What would life be like if God were insincere in His promises for today?

9. What would life be like if God were insincere in His plans for the future?

In verses 21 and 22 Paul identified three ministries God performs on our behalf that demonstrate His sincerity in His plans for the future. First, He establishes us in the faith. He gives us stability. He confirms us in our union with Christ. Second, He anointed us. God consecrated us to His service. Third, God sealed us. A seal signifies a finished transaction. God saved us once and for all; our salvation is an eternal, unchanging fact. A seal implies ownership. God has clearly identified us as His own property. We belong to Him forever. A seal also expresses security. The Holy Spirit is our seal; therefore, we are secure forever in His care.

10. How can believers show they are grateful for eternal membership in God's family?

Beginning in verse 23, Paul mentioned another reason he had not gone to Corinth: he wanted to give the church time to discipline a man who had committed incest by having an affair with his father's wife (1 Corinthians 5:1). Paul intended to delay his arrival to "spare" the Corinthians (2 Corinthians 1:23). He did not have absolute power over the Corinthians (v. 24) and did not want to visit them as a disciplinarian (2:1). Instead he intended to help them. His intentions were born out of love.

11. What evidence did Paul give of his love for the Corinthians (2:4)?

In love, Paul instructed the Corinthians about further dealings with the one who had "caused grief" (v. 5). Likely the woman in the illicit relationship was the offender's stepmother. In all probability the offender's father was still living when the offense occurred. In his first letter to the church at Corinth, Paul had told the believers to discontinue fellowship with the man. He had commanded, "Put away from among yourselves that wicked person" (1 Corinthians 5:13).

12. According to Matthew 18:15 and Galatians 6:1, what should be the goal of exercising church discipline?

13. What attitude should accompany this discipline?

Church discipline should purge sin and restore the sinner. Appropriately, then, the church in Corinth disciplined the offending member. Paul acknowledged this discipline when he wrote, "Sufficient to such a man is this punishment, which was inflicted of many" (2 Corinthians 2:6). The discipline had produced the desired result: the man had repented and turned his back on his sin.

14. According to 2 Corinthians 2:7 and 8, how should a church respond to a disciplined member who repents?

15. What would the Corinthians prove by forgiving the sincerely repentant believer (vv. 9, 10)?

In exercising church discipline, Christians must be extra careful lest Satan "get an advantage" of them by using one of his many devices or well-constructed plans (v. 11). Often Satan tries to make the hearts of church members cold and unforgiving so they will not restore offenders.

In verses 12 and 13 Paul demonstrated his sincere concern for the Corinthians by recalling the visit he made to Troas after leaving Ephesus. He intended to meet Titus in Troas, and he anxiously waited there for Titus's report on the church at Corinth. While waiting, he enjoyed excellent opportunities to preach, but he was restless in waiting to hear from Titus. He left Troas and traveled northwest to Macedonia (northern Greece), where he found Titus (2 Corinthians 7).

16. How do you think the Corinthians felt after reading that Paul had left opportunities to share the gospel so he could more speedily hear how they were doing?

17. In Whom did Paul place his confidence for victory (2:14)?

In verses 14–16 Paul illustrated the continual triumph of the gospel of Christ by comparing it to a triumphant military parade. The Corinthian believers must have clearly understood this imagery because they were familiar with the custom of a victorious army's parading through the streets and leading its captives along.

In his *Addresses on the Second Epistle to the Corinthians,* H. A. Ironside explained:

> When a Roman general had been out into some distant land to put down an uprising, or to win new lands for the Roman empire, to defeat great armies, the senate frequently voted him "a triumph." When he and his army returned to Rome, a public holiday was declared, and all the people thronged to the main thoroughfare to see this general enter in triumph. Here is a long line of captives, representatives of the people he has subjugated. They are in chains, and are holding censers in their hands, and

sweet fragrant incense arises. Then comes the general, and behind him another long line of captives bearing censers. These in
front are to be set at liberty, and the fragrant incense is the odor
of life unto them. Those behind are condemned to die, and are
going to the arena; they are to be thrown to the wild beasts or
put to death in some other way, and the fragrant incense that
arises from their censers is a savor of death. The general march-
es on in triumph. There are some with a savor of life, there are
others with a savor of death.

Where do you fit into this picture? Have you trusted in Christ as
your Savior? Are you sharing the gospel? Are you rejecting the gospel?

At the end of Paul's illustration, he reaffirmed his sincerity (v. 17)
and reiterated that he ministered "in the sight of God."

18. a. How does a person ensure that he or she is living in God's
eyes and not in the eyes of others?

b. When criticism comes, what difference does living "in the
sight of God" make?

Making It Personal

Follow Paul's example. Live in such a way this week that your testimony will amply reply to any accusations anyone might bring against
you.

19. a. If you were accused of being insincere, would the accusation have credence? Yes   No

     b. Why or why not?

20. What steps will you take to show sincerity in all areas of your life?

Sometimes Christians say things without meaning them or make promises they don't intend to fulfill. For example, it is easy to say, "Praise the Lord"; but do we truly mean it? It is also easy to say, "I will be praying for you" without our actually praying for that person.

21. What other sayings may be insincere or glib?

22. For whom will you pray sincerely, having promised to pray for that person?

23. Commit 2 Corinthians 2:17 to memory. Write the verse on the next page.

Lesson 3

Give Me Liberty!

2 Corinthians 3

"Now the Lord is that Spirit: and where the Spirit of the Lord is, there is liberty" (2 Corinthians 3:17).

Led by the United States, brave, free nations around the world battle despotism and terrorism. As they do so, we learn how privileged we are to enjoy liberty, and we long for others to experience it.

Getting Started

1. What comes to your mind when you hear the word "liberty"?

Freedom

2. Why do you cherish liberty?

Because we have freedom to Worship

Searching the Scriptures

Some of Paul's critics in the Corinthian church claimed that Paul was not a true apostle because he did not have letters of recommendation from the apostles in Jerusalem. Others said that he went around bragging about himself. Paul had to deal with these charges. He answered the accusation of fickleness by stating that he was sincere. But then some of his critics accused him of bragging! So he asked, "Do we begin again to commend ourselves?" (3:1). The answer was no.

Then Paul asked if he needed letters of recommendation to give the Corinthians. He had started the church of Corinth and was their founding pastor. Of course the church did not need letters of recommendation for him!

3. Read Acts 18:24–27. Whom did the church at Ephesus recommend by letter to the church at Corinth? (Corinth is in Achaia.)

4. What is the best recommendation a pastor can have?

5. Whom did Paul claim as his letters of recommendation (2 Corinthians 3:2)?

In these epistles, or letters (v. 3), Christ was the author; Paul, Silas, and Timothy were the pens; the Holy Spirit was the ink; and the hearts of the believers were the paper. The believers in Corinth were living letters. Anyone in that pagan city who saw the changes in the believers' lives could tell that Paul spoke with apostolic authority.

6. Read 1 Corinthians 6:9–11. How obvious would the change in the Corinthians' lives have been to the lost around them?

7. What should our family members, friends, neighbors, and associates be able to read clearly in our lives?

While the Corinthians were Paul's letters of recommendation, his credentials had come directly from Christ. Paul wrote, "And such trust have we through Christ to God-ward" (2 Corinthians 3:4).

8. Read Acts 9:11–15 and 22:17 and 21. What had the Lord commissioned Paul to be?

Paul strengthened his case in 2 Corinthians 3:5. He said, "Not that we are sufficient of ourselves." The word "sufficient" means "qualified." Paul freely admitted that in himself he was unqualified to do the task set before him, but he added, "our sufficiency is of [our qualification comes from] God."

In verse 6 Paul further affirmed that God had qualified him to be a minister of the New Covenant.

Paul's adversaries at Corinth and elsewhere were the Judaizers, Jews who professed to be followers of Jesus but who exalted the law of Moses. They wanted to bring Gentiles under the law. They insisted that a person could not be saved unless he or she kept the whole law. They denied salvation by faith alone.

The Judaizers had troubled Paul before. Seven or eight years earlier when Paul and Barnabas had been teaching in the church in Antioch,

Judaizers caused strife and nearly caused the church to split. Paul and Barnabas had to go to Jerusalem to meet with the apostles to settle the matter. The apostles called the first church council (Jerusalem, AD 50) to discuss the issue. The council, led by the Spirit of God, declared that Gentiles are not under the law of Moses and that salvation is by grace alone.

9. What verses of Scripture can you refer to that teach that salvation is by grace through faith?

The Judaizers, however, did not listen to the church leaders. They continued to disrupt churches and attack Paul. For that reason Paul had to write 2 Corinthians and defend himself against their charges. In the remainder of chapter 3, Paul showed that the New Covenant is better than the Old.

10. Read 2 Corinthians 3:6. What does the New Covenant of grace give that the law could never give?

11. Read verses 7 and 8. What did Paul call the ministration of the law?

12. What did he call the ministration of the Spirit (v. 9)?

God made a covenant with the nation of Israel. We call it the Old, or Mosaic, Covenant. It operated during the Dispensation of the Law[*] and was contained in a written code of laws. God introduced the "new testament," or New Covenant, by the shedding of Christ's blood (Matthew 26:27, 28; 1 Corinthians 11:25). By grace, the Holy Spirit energizes the New Covenant and writes it in the hearts of all who believe in Christ (2 Corinthians 3:3, 6).

Under the Old Covenant the human race was condemned to die because of sin. The law could point out sin, but it could not give people power to live victoriously over it. Under the New Covenant the Spirit of God comes to dwell in the heart of the believer, producing new life and providing new power whereby he or she can vanquish sin.

13. Read Romans 8:1–4. What does the Spirit accomplish in the lives of all who are set free from the law?

14. What would you tell someone who believes people must follow certain rules to gain favor with God (e.g., dress code, tithing)?

[*] A "dispensation" is "a mode of dealing, an arrangement, or administration of affairs." In the Dispensation of the Law, God dealt with mankind through the law of Moses. The way God administered the affairs of mankind changed from one dispensation to the next. Today we live in the Dispensation of Grace, because God is dealing with us through grace, not law.

The New Covenant is more glorious than the Old. The Old had some glory (2 Corinthians 3:7), but its glory paled in comparison to the glory of the New Covenant. While the Old Covenant given through Moses was glorious, the New Covenant that comes through Christ is "much more" glorious (vv. 9, 11).

In verses 12–18 Paul gave still more contrasts between the Old Covenant of law, given by Moses, and the New Covenant of grace, given by Jesus Christ. These verses show that the Old Covenant was temporary, while the New Covenant is permanent.

We often get the idea that Moses wore a veil because his face was so bright (vv. 11, 13). In reality, however, he did not wear the veil while he spoke to the Children of Israel. He put it on *after* he had spoken to them so they could not see the glory fade away (v. 13; see Exodus 34:29–35).

15. Moses hid his face to hide the fading glory of the Old Covenant (2 Corinthians 3:13). What should we do with the glory of the New Covenant (v. 12)? ("Plainness" means "boldness.")

Paul affirmed that the Israelites in Moses' day did not understand the significance of the fading glory of the law. They were in the dark, and the Jews of Paul's day were still there. They failed to see that the Old Covenant had ceased in Christ (vv. 14, 15).

Verse 16 indicates that one day Israel "shall turn to the Lord"; then "the [veil] shall be taken away." This will happen at the end of the tribulation period. Paul described this event in Romans 11:26 and 27: "So all Israel shall be saved: as it is written, There shall come out of Sion the Deliverer, and shall turn away ungodliness from Jacob: For this is my covenant unto them, when I shall take away their sins."

Salvation does not come by keeping the law. No one is ever saved by keeping rules. Salvation comes by placing our faith in Jesus Christ.

When the Philippian jailer asked the apostle Paul, "What must I do to be saved?" (Acts 16:30), Paul replied, "Believe on the Lord Jesus Christ, and thou shalt be saved" (v. 31).

The world reflects numerous groups of people. Some groups are national; others racial, some social, some religious, some political, and others economic. Such things as interests, pastimes, and spending habits can distinguish these groups further. But from the divine perspective, only two groups exist: those who depend on their good works to save them and those who rely on Christ alone. The good-works individuals are enslaved. The saved-by-grace individuals are free. However, even those who have received liberty in Christ need to understand that they must use their liberty in ways that honor Christ. We are not free to sin; we are free to do God's will.

16. What opportunities does liberty in Christ afford the believer?

17. What limitations come with liberty in Christ?

Making It Personal

18. What have the lost around you learned about God from your conduct?

19. What adjustments, if any, do you need to make so your life better communicates the hope of the gospel?

20. What will you do this week to help a good-works-for-salvation advocate realize his or her need to be saved by grace?

21. Commit 2 Corinthians 3:17 to memory. Write the verse below.

Hidden Treasure

2 Corinthians 4

"For God, who commanded the light to shine out of darkness, hath shined in our hearts, to give the light of the knowledge of the glory of God in the face of Jesus Christ. But we have this treasure in earthen vessels, that the excellency of the power may be of God, and not of us" (2 Corinthians 4:6, 7).

One day Muhammad adh-Dhib, a Bedouin Arab boy, and a friend were taking care of goats in the barren land eight miles south of Jericho. High bluffs overlook this region that stretches to the Dead Sea. One of the goats had gone astray, and the shepherd decided to look for it in nearby caves. The two boys threw a rock into one of the caves. Instead of hearing the usual sound of a rock hitting a stone wall, they heard a crash like the shattering of a jar.

That night the two boys looked inside the cave and found eight large jars. Seven were empty, but the eighth was sealed with pitch. Upon opening the sealed jar, they found three scrolls. They sold the scrolls to a manuscript dealer for less than $200.

At first even the manuscript dealer did not realize that the scrolls were treasures, but eventually several scholars saw the manuscripts and determined that they were extremely old. Then archaeologists began to search in earnest around Qumran near the Dead Sea. Years later, four scrolls from the area were sold for $250,000!

Over several years, about five hundred Dead Sea Scrolls were found. The scrolls contain parts of Exodus, Leviticus, Numbers, and Deuteronomy and the complete book of Isaiah. These manuscripts are about a thousand years older than any other Old Testament manuscripts.

These treasures were placed in clay pots covered with pitch. Because of these insignificant clay pots, the precious treasure was preserved for two thousand years. In 2 Corinthians 4 Paul talked about another treasure contained in "earthen vessels."

Getting Started

1. What valuable discovery have you made, perhaps at a garage sale or flea market?

2. a. What do you consider the most valuable item you own?

My rings, Home, Family I would say is the most valuable

b. What makes it valuable to you?

Searching the Scriptures

Second Corinthians 4 begins with a reference to Paul's perseverance. "We faint not," he wrote (v. 1). In spite of all the hardships that befell him as he preached the gospel from city to city in the Roman world, he did not give up.

Paul could have praised himself for his sacrificial nature. Instead he noted that he experienced difficult circumstances because of God's mercy. Mercy is the act of sparing someone the punishment he or she rightly deserves.

3. What did Paul escape through God's mercy that is far worse than any persecution he experienced as a minister (John 3:15–18)?

Being seperated from God forever. We all ehope that when we accept Christ as our Saviour.

Paul kept in mind the great kindness God had shown to him by giving him the privilege of ministering on His behalf. He wrote, "Seeing we have this ministry, we faint not" (2 Corinthians 4:1).

4. Every believer has received a ministry. What motivates you to perform your ministry even in the face of criticism or weariness?

Knowing it is what God wants me to do.

Paul explained that he had "renounced the hidden things of dishonesty" (v. 2). His life was open and genuine. He backed his word by his walk; he did what he said. Furthermore, his motives were pure. He did not walk "in craftiness" (v. 2). He was not an opportunist, shrewdly seeking to profit personally from the gospel. He did not "[handle] the word of God deceitfully" (v. 2). In other words, he did not alter the Word to gain a following or a fortune.

5. What deceitful use of the Word of God have you observed?

people getting rich preaching the word

In verse 4 Paul called Satan the "god of this world." "World" in this verse does not identify the physical world but the evil world system. Satan energizes the evil world system and rules over it. He works through unregenerate men and women in an attempt to thwart God's will.

6. What does Satan do to the minds of unregenerate people (v. 4)?

Satan tries to snatch away the Word of God before it sinks in and takes root. As a result, unbelievers remain in unbelief. It is an unending cycle: unbelief causes blindness, and blindness causes unbelief. Only the Spirit of God can break through and let the light shine in.

7. What are some means Satan uses to blind the minds of the unsaved?

8. What evidence have you seen of Satan's blinding the minds of the unregenerate?

In 2 Corinthians 4:5 and 6 Paul described his preaching.

9. Who was the focus of Paul's preaching (v. 5)?

Although Paul's enemies falsely accused him of being self-centered, he was truly Christ-centered. He proclaimed not himself but Jesus Christ.

10. What characterizes the life of a Christian who preaches him- or herself?

In addition to serving God, Paul sought to serve God's people. This goal was in keeping with Jesus' teaching. Jesus said, "Whosoever will be great among you, let him be your minister" (Matthew 20:26).

11. a. Name some people whom you consider great Christian leaders.

   b. What makes them great?

Paul affirmed that God "commanded the light to shine out of darkness" (2 Corinthians 4:6). At the beginning of time, God created light (Genesis 1:3). When He saved us, God enlightened our hearts (Ephesians 1:18; 5:8; 1 Peter 2:9). This spiritual illumination is as much a divine miracle as the miracle of creating light at the beginning of time. Dispelling the darkness cast by Satan over our minds and hearts is an action only God can perform. He gives us "the light of the knowledge of the glory of God in the face of Jesus Christ" (2 Corinthians 4:6).

Many unsaved people assume that the Christian life is dull, but Paul used "glory" and "light" to describe what God accomplishes in the lives of those who believe on Christ.

12. How has knowing Christ as Savior brightened your life?

In verse 7 Paul wrote, "But we have this treasure in earthen vessels." By "treasure" he most likely meant either the knowledge of God or the gospel ministry. *Both* are truly treasures.

In ancient times, artisans crafted vessels out of precious metals. When Nebuchadnezzar destroyed Jerusalem, he took many vessels of gold and silver from the temple and carried them away to Babylon. The vessels were highly valuable treasures. But the ancients also fashioned vessels out of clay. Those earthen vessels were inexpensive and fragile. They deteriorated easily. They were brittle. But they were used far more often than gold and silver vessels.

Our weak and deteriorating bodies are the earthen vessels that carry the treasure of the gospel by which we can know God. Few Christians are famous, wealthy, or powerbrokers. Most of us are simply unassuming people whom God uses to communicate the gospel of His glory to blinded men and women.

There is nothing attractive about the package that contains the gospel. The attractiveness comes from the gospel, which shines through the container. In 2 Corinthians 12:10 Paul taught that when we are weak, we are strong because God's strength is made perfect in weakness. The most effective instrument of God is not the most handsome, wealthy, or brilliant person but the person most yielded to God.

13. According to 1 Corinthians 1:26–31, why does God choose mainly average people to do His work?

So no person can glory from in His presence.

14. How does knowing that God most often uses average people to do His work encourage you?

I know I can do it

In 2 Corinthians 4:8–11 Paul reported difficulties of the ministry. He was "troubled on every side," meaning he was under constant pressure; but he was "not distressed." He was not crushed. He was not totally hemmed in without any way of escape. Paul was also "perplexed."

Sometimes he didn't know where to turn, but he was never "in despair." He was also "persecuted." His enemies pursued him, but God did not forsake him. God did not abandon him to the foe.

Further, Paul was "cast down." The term speaks of being temporarily defeated, of losing a battle. But Paul was "not destroyed." He lost some battles, but through God's help he was winning the war. He was down but not out.

15. a. Is it possible to proclaim the gospel and not be persecuted? Yes (No)

b. Why or why not?

Any time you proclaim the Lord or if people know you follow Christ they have something to say.

16. a. Have you experienced God's encouragement when you were discouraged? (Yes) No

b. How did He encourage you?

I always do. There have been so many times I would take all clos time

Verses 10 and 11 give a final contrast of the weaknesses and hardships the minister of the gospel experiences. These verses could be summarized to parallel the earlier four contrasts: "Always dying, but never dead." Paul was in constant danger. His life always hung by a thread because of his missionary work for Jesus.

Paul faced many troubles and trials, but his confidence in God remained unshaken. He knew beyond a doubt that God had raised Jesus from the dead and that He would raise him and the Corinthian believers from the dead as well (vv. 12–14).

17. a. What did Paul say would sustain him during his ministry (v. 15)?

The Grace of God

b. What would be the result?

Giving God thanks + glory.

In verse 16 Paul again stated his key thought: we do not lose heart. Paul could have gone down in despair because of all the trouble and trials in his life, but he did not despair. Instead he maintained his hope in God. In part, he based this hope on the resurrection of the dead.

In verses 17 and 18 Paul contrasted the temporary nature of his trials with the eternal values that motivated him.

18. Contrast what Paul said about his afflictions in verses 8 and 9 with what he said about them in verse 17.

In 8 + 9 He talked about his affliction + what they had done to Him. In 17 He described them as no big deal because eternal life is far greater.

19. What made Paul's afflictions seem light when they were actually extremely difficult (v. 17)?

He knew the reward in store for Him.

Paul's forward gaze beyond the end of his life to eternity made all the difference for him. Nothing he faced on earth could tarnish his hopes and curtail his perseverance. Paul found his hope in the eternal, in the as-yet unseen (v. 18).

Making It Personal

20. With whom have you recently shared your treasure, the gospel?

21. What fears motivate you to keep your treasure hidden from those who desperately need it?

I don't have any. I love Talking about Him

22. What truths can help you focus on eternal things rather than temporal things? *I Know God is truth and He tells me to hang in there Trust Him live + work for Him. I have eternal life full of blessings*

23. What one person will you commit to sharing your treasure with this week? *who ever comes my way*

24. Commit 2 Corinthians 4:6 and 7 to memory. Write the verses below.

6 For God who said "Let light shine out of darkness" made this light shine in our hearts, to give us the light of the Knowledge of the glory of God in the Face of Christ

7 - But we have this treasure in jars of clay to show that this all surpassing power is from God and not from us.

A Change of Address

2 Corinthians 5:1–15

"For we know that if our earthly house of this tabernacle were dissolved, we have a building of God, an house not made with hands, eternal in the heavens" (2 Corinthians 5:1).

Thirty-five years ago, John and Sara chose a lot on which a local builder built the house of their dreams. A few months prior to moving into their house, John and Sara selected the exterior paint colors, carpeting, cabinets, and lighting. When they moved into the house, they furnished and decorated according to their personal taste. As far as they were concerned, their house was perfect. It was attractive and comfortable.

Time and weather have changed John and Sara's house over the years. Today the outside shows signs of aging. The roof sags; the shutters look loose; the paint is dull; and the window trim is rotting. The interior, too, is showing signs of aging. The furnace doesn't work efficiently; often the plumbing becomes clogged; the carpet is almost paper thin; the walls are cracking.

John and Sara know the house has served them well for thirty-five years, and they realize that their finances and health are ill equipped to restore the old place to its original condition. So they are leaving it behind in a month or so. A new, maintenance-free home is waiting for them. Their son built it at no cost to them. They are understandably excited about the imminent change of address and their new home.

In 2 Corinthians 5 the apostle Paul wrote about a change of address that awaits every child of God. Someday each of us will leave the old "house" behind in anticipation of a far better, maintenance-free one.

Getting Started

1. If you have moved, what was the hardest part of moving from one residence to another?

Leaving my neighbors all the memories in the old house

2. What made the new residence so attractive?

Just the excitement

Searching the Scriptures

Paul was an experienced tentmaker, so it is appropriate that he referred to our bodies as tents ("tabernacle"; 2 Corinthians 5:1). A tent is a rather unstable structure. Most campers who have pitched a tent know how quickly a strong wind can take it down and even blow it away. Because a tent is fragile and fairly uncomfortable, most people would not choose to make a tent their permanent home.

3. What comparisons can you draw between the human body and a tent?

It wears out. Storms of life can bring it down

4. What implications for daily living do you see in the fact that your body is called a tent?

Life puts a stress on our bodies

5. How did Paul describe our new home (v. 1)?

An eternal home not built by human hands.

Because God is the architect, our new home must be wonderful! It is "not made with hands." It is not a physical body as our present tent is; it is a spiritual body. It is "eternal in the heavens." We may live in this physical body fifty, seventy, ninety years, but that is nothing compared to our new home. We will live on in our spiritual, glorified bodies forever. The new body is made for life in Heaven. It is perfect and is perfectly adapted to the heavenly realm.

6. Read 1 Corinthians 15:51–53. What two words describe believers' new bodies? *imperishable*

7. a. What characteristic of the glorified body do you find most appealing? *immortality*
will not perish
will never die
will never be sick

   b. Why? *you get tired of being sick and taking medicine, shots etc*

Life in Heaven will be wonderful! But for now we must face the trials and struggles that are a part of life on this earth.

8. What evidence of struggle do you see recorded in 2 Corinthians 5:2–4? *We groan & are burdened*

Why do we groan? Why do we carry such a burden? Why do we have to die? The answers lie in our history. Sickness, sorrow, suffering, and death go back to the dawn of time, when our first parents, Adam and Eve, chose to disobey God. In the Garden of Eden they fell into sin and brought upon themselves and their descendants a curse under which the world struggles to this day (Genesis 2:17).

9. Read Romans 5:12 and 8:20–22. What two consequences of sin do these passages mention?

death & Bondage

Afflictions and troubles plague us. Deep within us we earnestly desire "to be clothed upon with our house which is from heaven" (2 Corinthians 5:2). We long for our spiritual, glorified bodies. In Romans 8:23 Paul repeated the same thought, saying, "We ourselves groan within ourselves, waiting for the adoption, to wit, the redemption of our body." The day we receive our new, glorified bodies will be great and wonderful. We will no longer be tempted by sin, and we will no longer be subject to death.

God has guaranteed that every believer will receive a glorified body. Paul wrote that He "hath given unto us the earnest of the Spirit" (2 Corinthians 5:5). An earnest is a first installment, a down payment, a pledge of more to come. God makes this down payment at the moment of salvation, when the Spirit comes to dwell in the believer. He will never leave us. He will stay with us until we receive our glorified bodies.

10. What business transactions require earnest money?

11. What happens when a person backs out of a business transaction after paying earnest money?

12. Read Titus 1:2. How do you know God will keep His pledge to give you a glorified body?

13. Read 2 Corinthians 5:6–8. How do you know that when a Christian dies, he or she goes directly into Christ's presence?

While we are in these "tents" and "at home in the body," we should live for the Lord. The second half of 2 Corinthians 5 gives **five reasons.** The **first** is to please God. Paul said, "Wherefore we labour, that, whether present or absent, we may be accepted of him" (2 Corinthians 5:9). Pleasing God consumed Paul's life.

14. How would your life change if you could *see* God with you every moment of your life?

Notice that Paul was determined to please God whether he was still on earth or in Heaven. Paul must have deeply sensed God's presence in his life, for he determined to please God though he could not see or hear Him. Believers who postpone pleasing God will find that it is too late when they see Christ face-to-face.

The **second** reason we should live for the Lord is that we will all stand before Him at His Judgment Seat (v. 10) and receive rewards for faithful service. Christ will bring our actions, as well as our motives, to light. This manifestation will cover everything in our lives "whether it be good or bad." The "bad" includes acts of service done with improper attitudes or for the wrong reasons.

15. What attitudes of service would negate a reward for service?

16. What motives for service would negate a reward for service?

Verse 11 gives us the **third** reason we should serve the Lord. Paul said, "knowing therefore the terror of the Lord." The word translated "terror" here is frequently found in the phrase "the fear of the Lord." It also means "reverential awe." We should want to serve the Lord because we revere Him, because we stand in awe of Him.

17. Peoples' fears influence what they serve. If someone does not fear God, what are some things he or she might fear?

18. What did Paul's fear of God motivate him to do (v. 11)?

Paul stated that "we are made manifest unto God" (v. 11). In other words, Paul had nothing to hide before God's all-knowing eyes. He also trusted that the Corinthians would know him for who he really was (vv. 12, 13).

Fourth, we should serve Christ because of the love of Christ (v. 14). Scholars debate whether Paul was referring to Christ's love for us or to our love for Christ. Perhaps it is best to see both. "We love him, because he first loved us" (1 John 4:19), and we ought to want to serve Him because He loved us so much. We also should want to serve Him because we love Him so much. Paul saw the love of Christ as the glue that constrained him, or held him together.

19. People serve what they love. If someone does not love God, what things might he or she love and therefore serve?

The **final** reason we should live for the Lord is to introduce unbelievers to Him (2 Corinthians 5:14, 15). Some unsaved people may never know about salvation through Christ unless we tell them.

20. How highly does God value every person (v. 15)?

21. Why does God save people (v. 15)?

Making It Personal

22. Review your service for the Lord over the past year. What motivations, if any, have kept you from serving the Lord?

23. a. Review the reasons to serve the Lord:

   • to please Him

- to prepare to stand before His judgment

- to revere Him

- to acknowledge His love

- to share Him because people are lost

b. Circle the reasons that you find highly motivating.

24. How can these five reasons motivate you to serve the Lord this week?

25. Commit 2 Corinthians 5:1 to memory. Write the verse below.

God's Diplomatic Corps

2 Corinthians 5:16—6:10

"Now then we are ambassadors for Christ, as though God did beseech you by us: we pray you in Christ's stead, be ye reconciled to God" (2 Corinthians 5:20).

C ute," "precious," "darling," and "sweet" are words most often used by women, especially when they see a baby. Most people marvel at the new life reflected in a baby's cries, wiggles, and facial expressions. It is hard to hold a newborn and deny the existence of God. His creative power and infinite wisdom are so clearly reflected in that little bundle of joy!

His creative wonder and infinite wisdom are also reflected in everyone who has become His child through faith in Jesus Christ.

Getting Started

1. What thoughts about God come to mind when you see a baby?

2. What thoughts about God come to mind when you learn that
someone you know has become a child of God?

Searching the Scriptures

The apostle Paul told the Corinthians, "If any man be in Christ, he
is a new creature: old things are passed away; behold, all things are
become new" (2 Corinthians 5:17). Paul understood by personal experience and divine revelation that Christ is alive and able to save all who
trust in Him. According to verse 16, Paul once held a merely human
opinion of Christ, but that faulty perspective had changed dramatically.
He had come to know Christ by faith as His Savior.

In 2 Timothy 1:8–12 Paul gave his personal testimony, explaining
who saved him, how he was saved, what new direction his life had
taken, and what he was assured of.

3. According to 2 Timothy 1:8–12,

a. who saved Paul?

b. how was he saved?

c. what new direction did his life take?

d. what was he assured of?

The regeneration of a man or woman, boy or girl by the power of God is a miracle of divine grace. Paul used a word for "new" meaning "new in kind" in 2 Corinthians 5:17. When we are born again, we are changed into something drastically different from what we were. We receive a new nature from God, a new direction for life, and a new Sovereign to serve.

4. After you were born again, what changes did you notice

    a. in your attitudes?

    b. in your behavior?

Also in 2 Corinthians 5:17 Paul stated that "old things are passed away." What are these old things? The works of flesh found in Galatians 5:19–21—immorality, impurity, sensuality, idolatry, sorcery, strife, jealousy, a bad temper, selfishness, quarrelling, factions, envy, drunkenness, and carousing around—certainly passed from his life.

You might say, "But I know Christians whose lives manifest these 'old things.' " Yes, but those believers are not living up to their standing in Christ. They still need to learn to shun these bad attitudes and sinful habits, and surely they are not enslaved to them as they were before trusting in Christ. None of us have arrived at a sinless state. Although it is true that we are not as good as we ought to be, it is equally true that we are not as bad as we used to be.

5. Read Galatians 5:19–21. Which sins in these verses do you see occasionally in the lives of Christians, perhaps in your own life?

6. a. Which godly qualities listed in Galatians 5:22 and 23 do you see most prominently displayed in the lives of Christians?

b. Give one example of a godly quality you have seen recently.

As we study and obey God's Word and rely on the Holy Spirit for the power to lead a godly life, sinful habits and practices fade away and the fruit of the Spirit grows in us (Galatians 5:24, 25).

Believers are new creatures and can have the fruit of the Spirit because of reconciliation. The word "reconciliation" occurs five times in various forms in 2 Corinthians 5:18–20. "Reconciliation" means "bringing together."

7. What must two people do to be reconciled to one another?

8. Does God need reconciliation to individuals, or do individuals need reconciliation to God (v. 18)? Explain.

When Adam and Eve lived in the Garden of Eden, an extremely serious problem arose between God and the two humans because they turned their backs on God. They disobeyed God and fell into sin, severing their cordial relationship with God. Their sin separated them from God and placed them under divine judgment. However, God did not leave humans in their lost condition, although He would have been perfectly just to do so. In mercy He provided a temporary sacrifice, clothed our first parents in animal skins, and promised to provide a Redeemer (Genesis 3:15). In the fullness of time, He sent His Son, Jesus Christ, to die on the cross of Calvary to pay the penalty of our sin. Through Jesus' redemptive work, God "reconciled us to himself" (2 Corinthians 5:18).

9. How did Paul support the truth that God initiates and completes salvation (v. 18)?

In verse 19 Paul wrote that God not only reconciled us but also refused to impute our sins. In other words, He did not hold us accountable for our sins when He reconciled us to Himself. Because Jesus paid our account in full by shedding His blood for us, God cleared our account.

Suppose you fell on hard times and were $2,000 overdrawn at the bank and there was no way to come up with the money to cover the debt. You would have a serious problem, wouldn't you? But suppose further that someone covered the debt for you. Then you would be free and clear.

That is what Jesus did for us. We had a great debt of sin. We could not pay for it ourselves. Jesus paid for it by His death on Calvary. Verse 21 says, "For he [God] hath made him [Jesus] to be sin for us, who knew no sin." He took our debt and made it His own. He paid the penalty. When we trust in Him for salvation, our account is cleared.

10. What three words would you use to best describe Christ's death on the cross?

Suppose the person who cleared your debt did even more for you by transferring an incredibly large amount of money from his or her account to yours. Your account would then have a positive balance. According to the end of verse 21, God actually imparted His Son's righteousness to us. We have been "made the righteousness of God in him."

11. Is a Christian perfectly righteous in God's sight even when he or she doesn't feel righteous? Explain you answer.

As we look at the closing verses of 2 Corinthians 5, we learn that God gave us not only a righteousness but also a responsibility.

12. What responsibility did God give us (vv. 19, 20)?

13. What is involved in fulfilling this responsibility?

14. How well do you think Christians are generally fulfilling this responsibility?

Paul urged the Corinthian believers to act as ambassadors for Christ. He did not want them to ignore God's grace by being idle (2 Corinthians 6:1). When God extends His grace to a person, He admonishes him or her to join His diplomatic corps. He expects His people to work. Paul wanted the Corinthians to seize the present to invite people to be saved (v. 2). He and his coworkers had labored with God to proclaim the gospel, and they did so with pure motives (v. 3). Furthermore, Paul had modeled the rigorous life of an ambassador for Christ (vv. 4–10).

15. a. Who guided Paul into the afflictions, necessities, and distresses mentioned in verse 4?

  b. Which should the life of an ambassador for Christ reflect: a tourist on vacation or a soldier on a tour of duty? Explain.

16. a. Who inflicted Paul's stripes, imprisonments, and tumults (v. 5)?

  b. How should an ambassador for Christ expect to be received by a lost world?

17. a. Who instigated Paul's labors, "watchings" (sleeplessness), and "fastings" (v. 5)?

    b. How serious should an ambassador for Christ take his or her
       job? Explain.

18. What characterized Paul during his labor as an ambassador (vv. 6, 7)?

Paul endured misunderstandings and misinterpretations concerning his ministry as an ambassador. He dealt with them with patience because he kept his focus on Christ (vv. 8–10).

God has not canceled His call for ambassadors who are willing to risk their lives to carry His message of reconciliation to the lost. His diplomatic corps has room for many more men and women. Are you enlisted and on active duty?

Making It Personal

19. a. Suppose you received an evaluation from God on your role as an ambassador for Christ. What would the evaluation say?

b. What changes would God require?

20. a. To be an ambassador for Christ, you have to constantly build relationships with the "locals." What have you done recently to build relationships with the lost?

b. What more can you do to build relationships with the lost?

21. Commit 2 Corinthians 5:20 to memory. Write the verse below.

Dare to Be Different

2 Corinthians 6:11—7:1

"Be ye not unequally yoked together with unbelievers: for what fellowship hath righteousness with unrighteousness? and what communion hath light with darkness?" (2 Corinthians 6:14).

If you follow the news, you realize that a culture war is under way. An aggressive segment of society is using the media, public education, and the courts to try to squeeze everyone into one big tolerant mind-set. It is becoming increasingly unacceptable to hold distinct beliefs. We Christians are criticized for our exclusive beliefs that the Bible is God's fully inspired, reliable authority for faith and practice. We are ridiculed for believing that salvation comes through faith in Jesus Christ alone. Because we believe that the Bible condemns homosexuality, we are called homophobics and bigots. Even some religious denominations have allowed known homosexuals to serve as pastors and are legitimizing same-sex marriage. They say we all need to show love to those who are different. But how much do religious liberals and social engineers love believers who hold to different moral and doctrinal standards, those found in the Bible?

Getting Started

1. What intolerance have you recently observed in Christians?

The business meeting
The unwillingness to change

2. What do you think is the biggest difference between genuine Christianity and religious liberalism?

The way a person acts & lives.

3. How would you characterize Jesus' words, "No man cometh unto the Father, but by me" (John 14:6): exclusive or inclusive? Explain your answer.

You have to believe in Jesus Christ as the son of God to be saved.

Searching the Scriptures

Paul loved the Corinthians. He unmistakably communicated his affection for them. He wanted them to sense his deep longing for them through his letter.

4. Read 2 Corinthians 6:11 and the first part of verse 12. How did Paul communicate his love for the Corinthian believers? ("Not straitened in us" means "not restricted by us.")

He told them of his unrestricted openness in word and in heart

Conversely, the Corinthians *restricted* their love for Paul. When they should have been united with him, they pulled away from him (v. 12). Many of the Corinthians were suspicious of Paul's motives and character. They did not trust him.

5. How did Paul want the Corinthian believers to respond to his affection for them (v. 13)?

He wanted them to be open to him as he was to them.

Paul expected a father-child relationship with the Corinthians. After all, he had led many of them to Christ and was thereby their spiritual father. Paul desired to unite with the Corinthian believers in a way that should characterize relationships among believers today.

6. What strengthens the bonds among believers today?

praying to gether Sharing problem with each other.

7. What causes believers in a church to drift apart?

Bitterness, unforgiveness Gossiping ete

The Corinthians were not strongly allied with Paul. At the same time, they made alliances with those in error and with unbelievers. The apostle Paul warned the Corinthians, "Be ye not unequally yoked together with unbelievers" (2 Corinthians 6:14). He gave the reason for this command by presenting four nonnegotiable contrasts.

8. Read 2 Corinthians 6:14–16. What five contrasts did Paul cite?

Rightness & unrightness, light & darkness. Christ & belial Believer & unbelievers. The temple of God & unbelievers

9. Read Matthew 11:29. What yoke *should* believers carry?

Jesus Christ yoke

We cannot read Paul's admonition in 2 Corinthians 6:14–16 without realizing that we must not compromise our testimony to get along with evildoers. The life that honors God and the life that honors Satan are mutually exclusive. We cannot expect to mix the two more successfully than we would mix fire and gasoline. If we tried, we would surely get burned! If we hope to maintain distinction in our doctrine and lifestyle, we must apply the principle of separation. We must separate ourselves from wicked teachings and wicked behavior.

10. How comfortable are you with calling the following teachings wicked? Write "comfortable" or "uncomfortable" after each of the following teachings.

- The Bible is a fallible book written by men who communicated their religious experiences. _____

- God saves all who sincerely try to lead good lives. *Comfort able*

- Jesus was a truly good man, but He was not the Son of God. *uncomfortable*

- Jesus arose from the grave only in the sense that He lives on in the good deeds of His followers. *uncomfortable*

- We must put aside our religious differences and cooperate to build a better world. *comfortable*

- Hell doesn't exist. God would never punish human beings in such a place. *Comfortable*

To be dogmatic in today's social climate is frowned upon. However, believers must not soft-pedal truth to sound politically correct or to appease the tolerance crowd. We must recognize the insurgence of tolerance for sin and doctrinal error in the church and stamp it out.

11. What doctrinal beliefs do you consider foundational to Biblical Christianity? List at least five of these doctrines.

The Virgin Birth   He Will return
The Crucifixion of Jesus
His resurrection
He never Sinned

The Bible applies the principle of separation not only to religious affiliations but also to marriage. A believer should not marry an unbeliever. The two are incompatible in many areas of life. Since dating is the first step in selecting a marriage partner, this prohibition also applies to dating. A Christian should not date a non-Christian. Paul asked what agreement a believer has with an unbeliever (v. 15). Centuries earlier the prophet Amos asked a pertinent question that we may also apply to marriage: "Can two walk together, except they be agreed?" (Amos 3:3).

12. What consequences are likely in an unequally yoked marriage?

You will argue over the Kids you finances, The Christan will not go to church much.

13. What positive steps might a believer take to win his or her spouse to Christ?

Don't argue about it, pray for your spouse. Live your life the way God wants. Bea Kind + sweet.

Does the principle of separation apply to the business world also? The answer is a qualified yes. Paul taught believers that they should not withdraw from the world to the extent that they are totally out of it (1 Corinthians 5:9, 10), but Biblical principles certainly apply to the business world. Some Christians believe that the command not to be unequally yoked with unbelievers rules out having a business partnership with an unbeliever. Other Christians disagree, but we must recognize that in a joint business venture, the believer might be pressured to compromise his or her moral and ethical standards.

14. a. If you wanted to launch a business and a resourceful unbeliever wanted to be your business partner, what decision would you make?

Would not do it

b. Why?

Because that person would not pray + let God lead.

The principle of separation does not restrict us from working for a company where the boss or the owner is unsaved. In Paul's day many Christians worked for unsaved overlords. Paul's advice to them was not to run away but to be a good testimony (1 Timothy 6:1).

15. In what other areas might the principle of separation apply?

personal Time. Out side the business

Second Corinthians 6:17 commands, "Wherefore come out from among them, and be ye separate, saith the Lord." Clearly, infiltrating an apostate church or denomination in order to wield a Christian influence is an untenable policy. Paul did not advise us to go in but to come out!*

16. Did you leave an apostate church or denomination? If so, what persuaded you to leave?

Un Christian attitudes + actions

17. What counsel would you give those who believe they should stay in an apostate church and try to salvage it?

Leaving would let them know your belief is different

A believer loses nothing through separation. In fact, the separated life is the best life a believer can have.

18. What does God promise to those who separate themselves to Him (2 Corinthians 6:16–18)?

You will be close. Have a great fellowship.

Separation is *not* an end in itself. Those who practice separation for separation's sake will become self-righteous. Separation does not make a person more righteous; it improves his or her usefulness and brightens his or her light in a fallen world.

* If you would like to investigate this subject further, see "Is the Bride Unfaithful: Committing Spiritual Adultery by Joining with Unbelievers," *The Baptist Bulletin* (March 2005): 10.

19. Read 2 Corinthians 7:1. What should believers do in consideration of the promises God gives to those who practice separation?

Do away with anything that defiles the body or the spirit. Be they unto God.

20. Why is the fear of God a motivation for separation (v. 1)?

Because He will punish us.

Making It Personal

It is easier to separate from religious apostasy than from personal sinful habits. "Touch not the unclean thing," 2 Corinthians 6:17 commands. Living out that command takes a lifelong commitment to holiness and a humble reliance on God.

21. What should "[cleansing] ourselves from all filthiness of the flesh and spirit" (7:1) look like in your everyday life?

You should show a change

22. What changes do you need to make to practice personal separation from sin?

23. How can you separate yourself unto your Heavenly Father in such a way that you enjoy an intimate fellowship with Him?

Read His word more, pray more

24. Commit 2 Corinthians 6:14 to memory. Write the verse below.

Do not be yoked together with an unbeliever. For what do righteous + wickedness have in common Or what fellowship can light + darkness have with each other-

Lesson 8

Repentance Brings Relief

2 Corinthians 7:2–16

"For godly sorrow worketh repentance to salvation not to be repented of: but the sorrow of the world worketh death" (2 Corinthians 7:10).

I rrigation ditches channel much-needed water to farms, but when debris clogs those ditches, the flow of water may slow to a trickle or even stop. So farmers must inspect the ditches and work hard to clear away the debris. However, the increased water flow is worth the effort.

The flow of love from the Corinthians to Paul slowly trickled, but Paul worked hard to clear away misunderstandings and sins so their love would freely flow.

Getting Started

1. What relationships sometimes get obstructed?

2. a. Why does it take considerable effort to restore damaged relationships?

b. How should a person begin to restore a damaged relationship?

Searching the Scriptures

Paul confronted the Corinthians about immorality in their midst. In doing so, he provided a model for believers to follow in confronting fellow believers about their sins.

Paul wanted the Corinthians to open their hearts to him. "Receive us," he appealed to them (2 Corinthians 7:2). He wanted the Corinthians to make room in their hearts for him. Contrary to the rumors about him, he had lived blamelessly.

3. What negative actions did Paul say he had not committed (v. 2)?

4. Why must those who confront others be blameless?

Paul was not vindictive when he confronted believers. In fact, he loved the Corinthian believers dearly in spite of their standoffishness, and he had them in his heart. Railing on the Corinthians out of frustration was certainly a temptation Paul faced.

5. How deep was Paul's love for the Corinthians (v. 3)?

6. Why must a believer confront others out of a love-filled heart?

Verse 4 shows Paul's great joy after he heard from Titus that the Corinthians had responded in obedience to his first letter. He could then speak with confidence to others concerning them; he could be proud of them.

7. How did Paul describe the joy he felt when he heard the good news of the Corinthians' response to his letter (v. 4)?

8. What does a believer's rejoicing over another believer's sin and failure (1 Corinthians 13:6) reveal about that believer's heart?

Paul had written his confronting letter (1 Corinthians) in Ephesus; then he had gone to Troas, hoping to meet Titus after Titus delivered the letter. Not finding Titus at Troas, Paul went to Macedonia, hoping to meet him there. Paul wrote that his spirit was restless because Titus had not arrived (2 Corinthians 2:13). As long as Titus was absent, Paul had no way of knowing how the Corinthian church had received his last letter. In 2 Corinthians 7:5 Paul confided that he had had no rest in his flesh either. In other words, the matter had made him restless in soul and body. Paul revealed that "without were fightings, within were fears." Most likely he was referring to persecutions on the one hand and inner anxiety about the Corinthians on the other.

In due time Titus reached Paul and brought him good news concerning the Corinthian church: some believers were responding. While Paul received the good news from Titus, he looked beyond Titus to God, Who comforts the downcast (vv. 6, 7). When Titus and Paul met (probably in Philippi), Paul found that Titus had been encouraged by the Corinthians' strong desire to reconcile with Paul (v. 7).

After Paul sent his confronting letter, he had to leave the matter in God's hands. When Paul heard that the Corinthians had repented, God comforted him in that He had answered Paul's prayer concerning the Corinthians.

9. Why does a believer who confronts someone about his or her sin need to then leave the matter in God's hands?

Paul's letter to the Corinthians urging them to repent of their sin was strong and forthright. This frankness caused mixed emotions in Paul's heart.

10. What struggle did Paul experience after he sent his letter of confrontation to the Corinthians (v. 8)?

11. What does Paul's emotional struggle reveal about the difficulty of confronting a fellow believer?

12. What fears keep believers from confronting other believers about sin in their lives?

At some point after Paul wrote the letter and sent it on its way, he wondered if he had been too hard on the Corinthians (v. 8) or if they had become so entrenched in sin that they would not accept his teachings anymore. He regretted ever having sent the letter. Paul was obviously concerned about the manner in which he confronted the Corinthians.

13. What harm may come from a flippant rebuke or a hasty confrontation?

When Paul heard that the Corinthians repented, he no longer regretted sending the letter. Paul's purpose was not to lead them to grief but to lead them to repentance. He was glad he had made them sorry (v. 9). Furthermore, Paul wrote, "that ye might receive damage by us in nothing" (v. 9). In other words, Paul would not have to continue to deal with them sternly on the matter.

14. What happens when the person who confronts a believer continues to dredge up the sin even after the believer has repented?

Paul was glad not simply because the Corinthians were sorry but because their sorrow produced a genuine repentance of sin (v. 9). Being sorry is not enough. Repentance involves more than regret.

15. Name some people in the Bible who were sorry for their sins but did not repent. See, for instance, Genesis 4:8–15; 25:29–34; Matthew 27:3–5.

16. How does godly sorrow show in a person's life?

Godly sorrow leads to repentance, and repentance leads to salvation (v. 10). Worldly sorrow does not lead to salvation but rather to death.

17. Why do you think some people are unwilling to repent?

In verse 11 Paul used seven terms to describe the Corinthians' repentance.

First, "carefulness" denotes diligence. Earlier the Corinthian believers had been indifferent to the sin of the man guilty of incest. After receiving Paul's severe letter, they diligently dealt with the matter.

Second, "clearing of yourselves" indicates that the church had dealt with the sin and gave evidence of repentance.

Third, "indignation" reveals that the Corinthians were painfully aware of the shame brought upon their church by the sin in question.

Fourth, the word "fear" indicates that the Corinthians feared the wrath of God, which is poured out on sin. Perhaps they feared the consequences of the sin as it affected their church.

Fifth, "vehement desire" signifies a strong desire, or yearning for, something—perhaps a desire for Paul's favor and fellowship as the Corinthians had once known it.

Sixth, "zeal" describes the desire the Corinthians had to set things right and deal with the problem.

And, seventh, "revenge" suggests dealing out justice or punishment to the man guilty of incest. The Corinthians did so by removing him from the church. The Corinthians also seemed willing to accept any repercussions from tolerating the sin.

18. Go back through the characteristics of true repentance (v. 11) and summarize each one in a word or two.

True repentance involves a change of mind, recognition of wrongdoing, and renunciation of sin.

Paul closed verse 11 by concluding, "In all things ye have approved yourselves to be clear in this matter." Paul acquitted the Corinthians of any further responsibility in that case.

19. What reason did Paul give for writing his letter of confrontation (v. 12)?

20. What would the world say is more caring: glossing over a person's wrongdoings or confronting him or her about them?

The Corinthians' favorable response encouraged Paul. His joy doubled because Titus, too, was happy at their response. Paul had praised the Corinthians in front of Titus. Titus was then able to see that Paul's confidence in them had not been in vain (vv. 13–16).

Making It Personal

Does your Christian life cause your family, friends, and pastor to rejoice because you are responding to Biblical principles and Biblical teaching? Most important of all, does your life please God?

21. a. Do you practice true repentance?   Yes   No

b. Consider the following statements. Place a checkmark next to the statements that characterize your life.

___ I do not tolerate sin in my life.

___ I stay current in my relationship with God.

___ I have been victorious over a besetting sin.

___ I look at my past sins with regret and shame.

___ I respond humbly when confronted about my sin.

___ I diligently fill the void left by sin with obedience to God.

___ I seek to reconcile with those I have offended by my sin.

___ I actively take measures to avoid falling into the same sins.

___ I trust God for continued victory over sin.

___ I ask my spouse or a close friend to point out any sins he or she may see in my life.

22. From what sins, if any, do you need to truly repent today?

23. a. Do you properly confront fellow believers when they continue to practice sin?   Yes   No

    b. Consider the following statements. Place a checkmark next to the statements that characterize your life.

    ___ I do not gossip about other peoples' sins.

    ___ I regularly pray for those struggling for victory over sin.

    ___ I do not rejoice to hear about other peoples' sins.

    ___ I am motivated by love when confronting my sinning brother or sister.

    ___ I consider myself before approaching a fellow believer about his or her sin (Galatians 6:1).

    ___ I take time to craft my words carefully and prayerfully before confronting someone.

    ___ I do not jump to conclusions. I give the person I am confronting an opportunity to respond and explain him- or herself.

    ___ I do not give up on someone who refuses to repent (Matthew 18:15–17).

    ___ I offer a repentant believer my prayer support and my help.

    ___ I grant forgiveness with no strings attached.

24. What adjustments do you need to make in how or why you confront fellow believers?

25. Commit 2 Corinthians 7:10 to memory. Write the verse below.

Lesson 9

Charity Begins in the Heart

2 Corinthians 8:1–15

"For ye know the grace of our Lord Jesus Christ, that, though he was rich, yet for your sakes he became poor, that ye through his poverty might be rich" (2 Corinthians 8:9).

When Abraham gave Melchizedek, "priest of the most high God," a tenth of the spoils of his war to rescue Lot (Genesis 14:18–20), he did not give him money. Coins and paper money had not been invented. King Hezekiah, who died in 697 BC, never saw any money either. But about forty years later, King Gyges of Lydia in Asia Minor (modern Turkey) began to coin money out of electrum, an alloy of gold and silver.

By New Testament times people commonly used coins. We read of the widow's mite and of Peter's catching a fish with a coin in its mouth. However, the use of paper money was still far in the future. The Chinese invented it in AD 910.

At first money did not have the date of its minting stamped on it, but in AD 1234, a Danish bishop struck the first coins with dates attached. The Swedes also set a record when it comes to money: The heaviest coin ever struck was a Swedish 10 daler coin produced in 1644. It weighed 43 pounds 7.5 ounces.

85

We hardly pass a day without exchanging money. It is an inescapable part of modern life. In this lesson we will learn valuable principles concerning money.

Getting Started

1. If you suddenly inherited a million dollars, what plans for the money would initially come to your mind?

2. a. How much of the million dollars would you expect to give away?

b. To whom would you give it?

Searching the Scriptures

In the last chapter of 1 Corinthians, the apostle spoke of an offering he was going to collect from the churches of Galatia and from the church in Corinth to take to the church in Jerusalem (1 Corinthians 16:3). In 2 Corinthians 8 and 9 he raised this subject again.

Paul tried to motivate the Corinthians by citing examples of those who had already given to the relief effort. First he mentioned the Macedonians.

The Macedonians were extremely poor because the Romans had plundered Macedonia; yet, by the grace of God, they gave. Their giving reminds us of the poor widow who gave her mite. Jesus said that she had cast into the temple's treasury more than all that the rich people gave, for she had given all she had (Mark 12:41–44).

The Macedonians understandably could have complained about their poverty, but they did just the opposite. They had an abundance of joy even though they faced a great trial of affliction. They set a good example for the Corinthians and for us too. Our joy should not depend on our circumstances, but on the Lord. It takes the grace of God to live this kind of joyful life.

3. What did the Macedonians demonstrate about their spiritual state by giving out of their financial poverty (2 Corinthians 8:2)?

The Macedonians gave sacrificially. Paul reported that they gave "to their power" and "beyond their power" (2 Corinthians 8:3). Perhaps they understood the plight of the poor saints in Jerusalem better than members of other churches did, since they were in deep poverty themselves.

Not only did they give sacrificially and willingly, but they also gave sincerely. They implored Paul to receive their gift and take it to Jerusalem (v. 4). Paul was obviously reluctant to take it. He had not expected the Macedonians to contribute so generously.

4. What did the Macedonians call their giving (v. 4)?

5. The word "fellowship" means "partnership" or "sharing together." How can giving to the Lord's work be a partnership?

6. What decision did the Macedonians make before they gave their financial gift (v. 5)?

Consecration and surrender to Christ lie at the heart of giving and helping others.

7. What does stingy giving say about a person's love for the Lord?

Like the Macedonians, the Corinthians realized what a grim state of affairs the believers in Jerusalem faced. They, too, had decided to send a relief offering to the church in Jerusalem. They had good intentions. In fact, they had actually begun to collect the offering. Titus had been instrumental in getting them started (v. 6).

Paul challenged them to think seriously about giving. The Corinthian believers had many graces, or spiritual gifts; Paul wanted the Corinthians to "abound in this grace [i.e., giving]" (v. 7).

8. According to verse 8, what would the Corinthians' generous giving prove?

Giving is a spiritual gift; in fact, Romans 12:8 lists it along with other spiritual gifts.

9. What happens when someone gives to the Lord's work out of his or her own strength instead of the Spirit's power and leading?

10. What would you say to those who believe that they do not have the spiritual gift of giving and therefore do not need to be concerned about giving?

11. How does the gift of giving manifest itself in the life of a believer?

Some believers have a special gift of being able to give a great deal to support the work of Christ. Others do not. Nevertheless, all believers are to give as the Lord prospers them (1 Corinthians 16:2).

The Corinthians were wealthy. The Jerusalem saints were poor; they had a need. How could the Corinthians say that they loved the believers in Judea if they would not give financially to help them in their dire need?

12. How might your church more effectively minister to needy believers?

13. What obligation, if any, does your church have to help needy strangers who knock on your church's door and ask for donations?

In 2 Corinthians 8:9 Paul reminded the Corinthians of Christ's example of giving. Jesus Christ, the Lord of Glory, became the servant of men and women. He left the riches of Heaven and was born in a stable. He never owned a business or even a house. When He made His triumphal entry into Jerusalem, He rode on a borrowed donkey. When He died, He left no will, for He possessed nothing but the clothes on His back. Even they were taken from Him in His final hours. He owned the universe but died a pauper. He came from Heaven to earth that we might go from earth to Heaven.

14. What do you think is an appropriate response to Jesus' sacrificial love and grace?

Paul again reminded the Corinthians that they had begun to take up an offering the previous year but had not finished it. He urged them to complete what they had started (2 Corinthians 8:10, 11).

15. a. What are common excuses for delaying one's giving to the Lord's work?

b. Are any of the excuses valid? Explain.

When Paul urged the Corinthians to give, he did not want to put a hardship on them so they in turn would be driven to poverty (v. 13).

He was not asking them to give according to what they did not have but according to what they had. Giving should be in proportion. So he urged them to give out of their abundance (v. 14) to help supply the needs of the Jewish believers in Jerusalem. He also reminded them that in time the situation might reverse. Someday the Jerusalem believers might have plenty, and the Corinthians might have little (v. 14). In that case Paul would expect the Jerusalem believers to send gifts to the Corinthians.

16. What do you think it would take to persuade materialistic Christians to put spiritual values ahead of materialistic interests?

17. Read Exodus 16:14–18. What incident did Paul refer to in 2 Corinthians 8:15 to motivate the Corinthians to give?

Paul was communicating to the Corinthians that all they owned had come from God. Their riches, like the manna from Heaven in the Old Testament, had come from God. God gives some people more so they can share with those who have less. Those who horde their money miss out, both now and in eternity, on the far greater blessings of giving.

Making It Personal

The apostle John shared with his readers the same truth Paul communicated to the Corinthians. In 1 John 3:17 and 18 John expressed doubt that God's love dwells in the person who enjoys material prosperity but ignores a fellow believer's need. He urged his readers to respond to the need with appropriate action.

18. What needy person or group of people could use your help this week?

19. How will you help that person or group? List specific ways.

20. Knowing that the Lord has given so much to you, including the sacrifice He made at Calvary, what will you offer Him today?

21. Commit 2 Corinthians 8:9 to memory. Write the verse below.

The Joy of Giving

2 Corinthians 8:16—9:15

"Every man according as he purposeth in his heart, so let him give; not grudgingly, or of necessity: for God loveth a cheerful giver" (2 Corinthians 9:7).

A disgruntled, miserly church member refused to partici-pate in an offering for missions. "I don't believe in missions," he muttered when an usher passed the offering plate to him.

"Then take something out," the usher replied; "it's for the heathen."

Perhaps a non-Christian would object to an offering, but every Christian should participate in offerings that support the Lord's work and minister to others.

Getting Started

1. What is the best gift you have received from a friend or family member?

2. What act or acts of giving have brought you great joy?

Searching the Scriptures

In 2 Corinthians 8:1–15 Paul encouraged the Corinthians to collect an offering for the poor believers in Jerusalem. Paul told the Corinthians that after the offering had been collected, it would need to be delivered to Jerusalem.

Paul found the perfect candidate in Titus. Titus had the same eagerness for the Corinthians' participation in the gift that Paul had for them (v. 16). Paul was thankful for this fact, and he encouraged Titus to go to Corinth to help organize the collection in that church. Titus was so eager to help that he volunteered and would have gone even if Paul had not asked him to do so (v. 17).

Paul also sent another Christian brother—perhaps Luke, Silas, Timothy, or Mark—to help collect this offering (v. 18). The third member of the team was a highly regarded person whom the Macedonian churches had appointed (v. 19). The three messengers were men of character who served the churches (v. 23).

3. Why was Paul wise to send more than one person to receive the offering (vv. 20–22)?

4. What guidelines do you think a church should follow in collecting and dispersing funds?

5. What character qualities should a congregation look for in those who handle their finances?

Since Titus was Paul's personal helper, and since the two other men were official messengers of the churches, Paul encouraged the Corinthians to show them the proof of their love (v. 24), that is, to demonstrate by their liberal gift that their love was genuine.

6. What correlation exists between a believer's giving and his or her love for the Lord?

Paul mentioned in 2 Corinthians 8:10 that the Corinthians had begun a year earlier to take up an offering. They had started well and had made the commitment to give. For this reason, Paul had referred to the Corinthians as a good example when he addressed the Macedonians, and the Corinthians' commitment had stirred the Macedonians to action (2 Corinthians 9:2).

7. How could your church discreetly use personal testimonies about giving to spur members to give?

Have you ever highly recommended someone for a job only to find that when the person was hired, he or she did not live up to the employer's expectations? Have you ever recommended a church only to find that things had changed and the church no longer stood where it once had? Either case would be quite embarrassing, to say the least.

Paul had boasted about the Corinthians to the believers in Macedonia (9:1, 2). He did not want the Macedonians to go to Corinth and find that the Corinthians had failed to complete what they had started (v. 3). If the Macedonians found the Corinthians unprepared, both Paul and the Corinthians would be embarrassed (v. 4).

So Paul sent Titus and two other believers to help the Corinthians prepare for a visit by Paul and some Macedonians. Titus was to help the Corinthians get their collection together so they would give out of generosity instead of "covetousness" or grudging obligation (v. 5).

Paul informed the Corinthians that bountiful givers receive a blessing (v. 6). He based this promise on an Old Testament principle of sowing and reaping found in Proverbs 11:24.

8. What did Jesus say about the blessing of giving (Acts 20:35)?

9. What are some blessings of giving?

10. Describe a time when giving brought blessing to your life.

In 2 Corinthians 9:7 Paul wrote, "Every man according as he purposeth in his heart, so let him give."

11. How much thought and planning should go into giving to the Lord's work?

Emotional giving often leads the giver to regret his or her rash action. Planned giving never does. Giving should be deliberate, not casual.

Furthermore, we should not give "grudgingly" (v. 7). This word denotes grief or sorrow. "Of necessity" indicates compulsion. Our giving should be neither reluctant nor obligatory. We should always give because we love the Lord.

After the Reformation, many parts of Europe established a state church to which every citizen of the country belonged. Officials collected dues for the church, much like they collected taxes for the state. Such a method of supporting the church certainly is unbiblical.

12. What does it mean to be a cheerful giver (v. 7)?

13. a. If you cannot give cheerfully, should you stop giving until you can be cheerful about it?   Yes   No

    b. Explain.

Paul did not say that God loves an exorbitant giver. Yet some Christians try to impress God with the amount they give to Him.

14. Why is it impossible for a person to please God by giving exorbitantly to His work without regard to his or her attitude?

15. Why must a giver be cheerful to please the Lord?

16. What does God promise to those who give cheerfully (v. 8)?

17. What motive for giving might the teaching "You cannot outgive God" appeal to? Why?

Notice that Paul did not say that the Corinthians would get more money back from God every time they gave money toward the offering, as if they could potentially make money by giving it to the Lord. Paul did say that God, by His *grace,* would supply their needs. No one deserves to get anything from God. *All* we have from God is a measure of His grace. We cannot expect God to abundantly fill our coffers because we give to Him regularly.

God has promised to meet all our needs (Matthew 6:33; Philippians 4:19), and "every good gift and every perfect gift" comes from Him (James 1:17). So our giving is a way to acknowledge His benevolent love and grace.

Paul explained that God supplies the seed for the sower and bread for food (2 Corinthians 9:10). He does this by sending rain for the crops, which increases the amount of seed to plant the next year and to eat during the present year. This supply results in thanksgiving to God (v. 11).

It was hard for Jewish believers to accept Gentile believers. But when they saw the gift from the Gentile believers, they would realize that the Gentiles were sincere in their beliefs. The Jewish believers would accordingly give thanks to God (v. 13).

18. How well does your giving to the Lord prove that you believe His Word?

19. Why would you expect the per-person rate of giving to be higher in a Bible-believing church than in a church that denies the fundamentals of the faith?

Because of the Corinthians' gift, the needs of the poor believers in Jerusalem would be met. The gift "supplieth the want [need] of the saints," Paul explained in 9:12. Meeting needs is a practical benefit of an offering. The Corinthians' gift would buy food and clothing for the poor believers in Jerusalem.

We may not think of giving as a ministry, but Paul did. He looked upon this giving as an important ministry by the Gentile churches to the Jewish church. The Jewish Christians in return would come to love the Gentile Christians and to pray for them (v. 14).

Paul closed this chapter by reminding believers that we should thank God for the greatest gift ever given, the gift of the Lord Jesus Christ (v. 15). In doing so, Paul reflected the central truth of the gospel: "For God so loved the world, that he gave his only begotten Son, that whosoever believeth in him should not perish, but have everlasting life" (John 3:16).

Making It Personal

20. What three words describe your giving to the Lord over the past year?

21. a. Are you cheerful when giving?   Yes   No

    b. If not, what is keeping you from being a cheerful giver?

    c. Ask the Lord for His grace to help you remove any obstacles that are keeping you from being a cheerful giver.

22. How often do you evaluate your giving?

23. Use the following exercise to help you evaluate your giving.

    a. Place a checkmark next to each statement that reflects your giving practices.

    ___ I pray about how God wants me to use His money.

    ___ I allow the Lord's leading rather than a certain percentage of my income to dictate my giving.

    ___ I give regularly at or above my planned giving amount.

    ___ I give to meet special needs as they arise.

    ___ I am willing to give up something in order to have more to give to the Lord.

    ___ I enjoy giving to the Lord.

    ___ I give to honor and glorify God.

    ___ I do not boast to others or to myself about how much I give.

    ___ When I receive extra income, I consult God about how to use it.

    b. Review the above list. In what ways, if any, does God want you to adjust your giving practices?

c. Respond to God's leading and enjoy the benefits of giving both now and for eternity!

24. Commit 2 Corinthians 9:7 to memory. Write the verse below.

Apostle in the Crosshairs

2 Corinthians 10

"But he that glorieth, let him glory in the Lord. For not he that commendeth himself is approved, but whom the Lord commendeth" (2 Corinthians 10:17, 18).

Jesus warned His disciples that they would encounter persecution and rejection. He said, "If the world hate you, ye know that it hated me before it hated you. . . . The servant is not greater than his lord. If they have persecuted me, they will also persecute you" (John 15:18, 20). The apostle Paul lived out both sides of Jesus' statements. Before becoming a believer, he despised Jesus and persecuted His followers. After he became a believer and an apostle of Jesus Christ, he was constantly a target in the enemy's crosshairs. He encountered rejection and persecution wherever he carried the gospel. Often those who opposed him most vehemently were the professed religious leaders.

Getting Started

1. Why is criticism easy to give but hard to take?

2. How has criticism affected your life? Are you better or worse because of criticism?

It makes me think more about how Jesus must have felt.

Searching the Scriptures

Paul's critics accused him of being a coward. They would have respected him more if he had been aggressive in their midst. They also accused him of being meek in their presence but bold in his letters. Then, as now, power-hungry church politicians find it hard to understand a meek, mild leader.

Because of the circumstances, Paul was forced to defend himself and use his apostolic authority, but he also wanted to follow the pattern of meekness that Christ exemplified. The Lord Jesus Christ refuted the misconception that meekness and gentleness are incompatible with sternness. He spoke as One having authority, yet He was meek and mild. For example, He was meek when He stood before Pilate. He did not flare up against the false charges that the Jewish leaders hurled against Him. On the other hand, He was forceful when the occasion called for it. For example, He called the Pharisees hypocrites to their faces. Meekness may seem like weakness, but it is not. It takes a strong person to remain meek in the face of opposition and provocation.

3. a. Do you find it hard, almost impossible, to be meek in the face of harsh criticism? (Yes) No

   b. If so, why?

It is so hard not to say something back.

4. Under what circumstances might it be wise to respond assertively to your critics?

When you feel it is you the cause of christ.

Paul began chapter 10 of 2 Corinthians with a tone of authority. He wrote, "I Paul myself." Paul defended himself personally because his critics had attacked him personally. Yet he did not become assertive simply to please them. Rather, he entreated them "by the meekness and gentleness of Christ" (v. 1).

In the second half of verse 1 and in verse 2 Paul revealed his ability to deal just as sternly with the Corinthians in their presence as he dealt with them in his letters.

Paul's critics also accused him of walking according to the flesh. Paul made a play on words by stating that he did "walk in the flesh" (v. 3); that is, he was a human being. He had a body with its limitations. Because he was human, he was weak. But, he told them, he did not use human weapons such as craftiness, deceit, or earthly wisdom (v. 4). Rather, he used powerful spiritual weapons that pull down the strongholds of false teaching. He used them to cast down "imaginations," or sinful human reasoning (v. 5).

5. What carnal weapons might a believer use in ministry?

6. What will happen to the ministry of a Christian who relies on carnal weapons to carry on his or her ministry?

It will not work

7. According to Ephesians 6:11–18, what spiritual weapons are available to believers?

> The armor of God defensive
> word of God + prayer offensive

8. What will happen to the ministry of a believer who relies on spiritual weapons to carry on his or her ministry?

> It will be great + will
> last.

False teachers often rely on systems of philosophy. Paul sought to capture men and women for Christ and to bring them into submission to Him. Paul offered the Corinthians a little more time. But after the majority obeyed the Word of God, he would bring to justice any minority who would not obey the truth (2 Corinthians 10:6).

The false teachers in Corinth were maligning Paul's character and underlining his authority. So Paul told the Corinthians to look at the facts. He believed that the details of his life would vindicate him. He could not have instructed the Corinthians to do this if his life were not open and above reproach.

Paul may have had a specific false teacher in mind. Apparently this false teacher thought he had a special relationship to Christ. Paul told him to think again and to remember that Paul, too, was rightfully a servant of Christ (v. 7).

9. Why is it a sin for a person to think he or she has a special relationship with Christ that makes him or her better than everyone else?

> When you think you are
> so special you are prideful
> + that is a sin.

10. Why is it a sin for a person to think he or she is deficient as a Christian and cannot measure up to anyone else?

When you feel sorry for yourself & go around brenging people down that is a sin

Paul then claimed that he would not feel ashamed of himself even if he were to boast a little more about his authority (v. 8).

11. For what reason did God give Paul authority (v. 8)?

To build up believers

12. What happens to a church whose pastor uses his authority to edify the believers?

The believers will go spiritualy & help each other

Paul explained that he was already using restraint in writing about himself (v. 9). In other words, he was using his God-given authority as he should. He refrained from destroying the Corinthians through verbal attack.

13. What was *not* a reason for God's giving authority to Paul (v. 8)?

To destroy the believers

Paul's enemies alleged that Paul could write stern letters as long as he remained at a distance. But they added that in person Paul would be weak and that his voice would be contemptible (v. 10). They came to those conclusions because in Corinth Paul had been mild. However, Paul had to be stern in his letters because of the divisions, immorality, and disorderly conduct in the Corinthian church. He assured the false teachers that he could be equally stern in person (v. 11).

14. When have you found it necessary to be stern for the sake of the gospel?

When I faced the false teacher at the hospital

In 2 Corinthians 10:12 Paul took the false teachers to task on another matter. He showed that his critics unwisely commended themselves. He defended his boldness but showed that he was not as bold as his opponents, who dared to rest their authority on self-recommendation. Such people formed cliques, set up their own standards, and then praised one another for having met those standards. That kind of reckless boldness was foreign to the apostle. He did not wish to add himself to their number or even to compare himself with them. He also warned them that commending themselves was downright foolish.

15. What is the harm in using each other as spiritual measuring sticks?

When we down others it pulls us down - cause it makes us feel bad.

Paul added that the Corinthians' faith commended him (vv. 14, 15). God had led him to Corinth. He had won the Corinthians to the Lord and had founded the church there. The Corinthians were his spiritual children. Paul reported in verse 14, "We are come as far as to you also in preaching the gospel of Christ."

In verse 15 we see a principle that Paul followed on his missionary journeys. He did not want to go where someone else had already gone. When he went to Corinth, it was virgin territory for the gospel; no one had yet reached there. After starting the church at Corinth, he desired to go to the "regions beyond" (v. 16). He did not want to boast in what another man had done. In fact, he hoped that the faith of the Corinthians would increase to the point where they would support him in his work to preach the gospel in new lands (vv. 15, 16).

16. Why might it be wrong for believers to abandon or ignore a church plant in order to join a large church that has more to offer them?

The false teachers had little interest in pioneer missionary work. They preferred to take over the works of others, "to boast in another man's line of things made ready to [their] hand." Paul would not boast in other men's works (v. 16). He believed that if a minister wanted to boast, he should boast in the Lord (v. 17).

The ultimate proof of Paul's apostolic authority came from the Lord Himself. His commendation was all the approval Paul needed. Self-commendation means nothing. The commendation of the Lord means everything (v. 18).

We need to live in such a way that God can commend us too. It matters little what others think of us or say about us. What matters most is what God thinks of us.

Making It Personal

17. How do you react when people criticize you for your service for the Lord?

18. What steps can you take to ensure a proper response the next time you are criticized for your ministry?

19. How supportive have you been of your pastor?

20. What can you do to show your pastor that you support his authority and edification ministry in the church?

21. Commit 2 Corinthians 10:17 and 18 to memory. Write the verses below.

Bragging Rights

2 Corinthians 11

"I say again, Let no man think me a fool; if otherwise, yet as a fool receive me, that I may boast myself a little" (2 Corinthians 11:16).

There's nothing like a hotly contested conference rivalry between college football teams. The final game to determine the conference champions generates high emotions and lots of media attention. Each team wants to win and thereby capture bragging rights—at least for a year.

In 2 Corinthians 11 the apostle Paul squared off against his critics. They charged that he was not an apostle. In his defense, Paul claimed bragging rights to his apostleship. However, he assured the Corinthians that he was playing the role of a fool in doing so. He simply wanted to make a strong point: he was as much an apostle as any of the other apostles.

Getting Started

1. What bragging rights can you claim?

2. What did you do to earn those bragging rights?

Searching the Scriptures

In chapter 11 of 2 Corinthians the apostle Paul acted like a fool, or at least he thought he acted like a fool. He said, "Bear with me a little in my folly" (v. 1). He felt uneasy about what he was going to do. He considered it foolish but necessary because of his loving, anxious concern for the Corinthian Christians. He appealed to his testimony as a way to counteract the impact of the false teachers.

Paul chose to write about himself because he was jealous over the Corinthians, as a father is jealous over his children (v. 2). He had begotten them through the gospel. Now they—as members of the Body, the Bride of Christ—were espoused (married) to Christ. Therefore, Paul wanted them to remain pure.

If you have led someone to saving faith in Christ and then discipled that person, you understand Paul's concern. Paul guarded the Corinthians' welfare carefully because they were in danger of being seduced into unfaithfulness by the false teachers who had invaded their community (v. 3).

Just as Satan's guile in the Garden of Eden led Eve astray, so false teachers sought to corrupt the minds of the Corinthians. False teachers tried to turn the Corinthians away from Paul and his teachings. This deviation would have turned them away from Christ as well.

3. Why is it important to disciple a new believer soon after his or her salvation?

The false teachers in Corinth had come into the church and were preaching "another Jesus" (v. 4). They taught that salvation depended upon faith plus works, insisting that the Corinthians keep the law of Moses. Paul called this doctrine "another gospel" (v. 4) and warned the Corinthians that their minds would be "corrupted from the simplicity that is in Christ" (v. 3).

4. How do you define the gospel?

5. According to 1 Corinthians 15:3 and 4, what are the key elements of the gospel?

Paul described himself as rude in speech but not in knowledge (2 Corinthians 11:6). He was an authority on the subject of salvation because his knowledge came by direct revelation from Jesus Christ (Galatians 1:12). What better source of knowledge could anyone have than Jesus Christ Himself?

6. A smooth-tongued orator usually gets more attention than a clumsy-tongued talker. What do people assume when they hear a smooth-tongued orator?

7. What was the one area in which Paul was not lacking (2 Corinthians 11:6)?

8. How would Paul counsel a Christian who wants to share his or her testimony even though he or she is not an outgoing, gifted communicator?

Paul received no financial support from the Corinthians while he worked to start the church in Corinth. Surely no one could criticize him for ministering free of charge. But his critics did. They claimed that Paul's refusal to take support from the Corinthians indicated a lack of love for them.

Paul answered this charge in 2 Corinthians 11:7. He asked if he had committed a sin in abasing himself. He was referring to his humbling himself by making tents for his own financial support.

9. According to 2 Corinthians 11:8, from whom did Paul receive financial support when he ministered in Corinth?

10. Why would Paul not ask new believers for money?

11. How should a church communicate principles of giving to a new believer without sounding money hungry?

Even in his times of need, Paul did not burden the Corinthians (v. 9). On the other hand, the false gospel preached in Corinth provided the

Judaizers with a livelihood. That provision put them at a disadvantage when they attacked Paul, for Paul did not receive any remuneration from the Corinthians for his preaching. Paul gloried in being able to preach in southern Greece (where Corinth was located) without cost to the people to whom he ministered.

The false teachers tried to turn Paul's ministry-without-pay policy against him by claiming he did not love the Corinthians. Paul answered this charge with a rhetorical question: "Wherefore?" In effect Paul asked, "Why did I not take your money? Because I did not love you?" The answer is "God knoweth" (v. 11). Paul loved the Corinthians dearly.

In verse 13 Paul unmasked his opponents, calling them "false apostles" and "deceitful workers." Although they passed themselves off as apostles of Christ, they were energized by the Devil. Today, too, many religious leaders who oppose Christ masquerade as His apostles. They are simply following the practice of their leader, the Devil.

12. What can a Christian do to make him- or herself distinct from false teachers?

Churches that openly scoff at the Bible still call themselves Christian. Their leaders call themselves pastors. They masquerade as heralds of truth. Satan is transformed into an angel of light (v. 14) and his servants into ministers of righteousness (v. 15). Paul wrote of them, "Whose end shall be according to their works" (v. 15). Christ will judge them according to their evil deeds, not according to their apostolic pretensions.

13. According to Matthew 7:15 and 24:11, how did Jesus describe false prophets?

In 2 Corinthians 11:16–18 Paul returned to writing about himself. He thought boasting was foolish; nevertheless, circumstances had forced him to compare his credentials with those of the false teachers. He asked the Corinthian believers to receive him even if they considered him a fool. The imposters had boasted about themselves, and the Corinthians had received them. So Paul decided that the time had come for him to boast also for a little while, even though he found boasting extremely disagreeable.

Before he started boasting, Paul pointed out to the Corinthians that the Judaizers were fools, yet the Corinthians, who thought themselves wise, believed the Judaizers to be wise (v. 19). Paul went on to list the abuses the Judaizers had inflicted on the Corinthians.

14. What did the Judaizers do to the believers in Corinth (v. 20)?

Paul began his boasting by detailing his pedigree (v. 22). Apparently his opponents were Palestinian Jews who boasted of the purity of their descent so they could convince the Corinthians they were true apostles. They took great pride in being Hebrews. They spoke Aramaic, the language of the Jews in Jerusalem. But Paul spoke it too. They boasted in being Israelites, being part of the Chosen Nation. But Paul was part of it too. They gloried in being of the seed of Abraham. But so was Paul. They were "true blood Jews," not converts from the Gentiles. But so was Paul.

Second, Paul boasted about his trials (vv. 23–28). Although the false teachers came from Jewish stock, they were not in the same class with Paul when it came to trials. Someone has said that the more a man suffers, the more he ministers. In any case, Paul was more of a minister of Christ because of what he had to suffer. He suffered a great deal of physical abuse from other people.

15. According to verses 23–28, what trials had Paul endured as an apostle?

16. a. Which trial do you think was the hardest to endure?

b. Why?

The trials Paul faced had not just started. He had faced them from the beginning of his ministry. Even back then his enemies had attempted to take his life (vv. 32, 33).

The false apostles in Corinth wanted a rich, easy, rewarding life. But Christ did not call His apostles to that kind of life. Paul's life of danger and hardship was in line with the lives of the other true apostles (compare Peter and John [Acts 4] and James [Acts 12:2]). Paul's life testified to his apostleship, and Paul used it in 2 Corinthians 11 as a defense against his attackers.

17. Why does enduring hardships for Christ strengthen a person's testimony as nothing else can?

18. What can believers do today to ensure a good testimony?

Making It Personal

Paul served as an outstanding example of love for Christ and fellow believers by putting ministry ahead of personal comfort. He resolutely proclaimed the gospel all the days of his life, and at the end of his life he testified, "I have fought a good fight, I have finished my course, I have kept the faith" (2 Timothy 4:7).

19. Place a checkmark next to the statement below that tells how well Paul's testimony in 2 Timothy 4:7 matches yours today.

____ The two match each other perfectly.

____ My testimony is close to matching Paul's.

____ My testimony falls far short of matching Paul's.

20. How can you strengthen your faith and Christian service so you will be able to echo Paul's testimony at the end of your life?

21. With whom will you share your testimony this week?

22. Commit 2 Corinthians 11:16 to memory. Write the verse below.

Ready or Not, Here I Come

2 Corinthians 12; 13

"And he said unto me, My grace is sufficient for thee: for my strength is made perfect in weakness. Most gladly therefore will I rather glory in my infirmities, that the power of Christ may rest upon me" (2 Corinthians 12:9).

Before the advent of television, children spent more time playing games such as Annie, Annie, Over; Tug of War; Red Rover; Crack the Whip; King of the Hill; Hopscotch; Leap Frog; Hide and Seek. In Hide and Seek, one child is "It" and the other children hide. "It" counts to fifty or one hundred and says, "Ready or not, here I come," meaning the other children have had all the time they are going to get to find places to hide. Now "It" is coming to search for them. If they have not done a good job of hiding themselves, they will soon be found out.

Paul had been dealing with the Corinthians in previous letters as well as in 2 Corinthians. Soon he would go to Corinth and hold the believers there accountable for their actions. He hoped and prayed that they would have their church in order when he arrived. Even if they did not, he would go there. If the church were not in order, he would have to deal with it firmly. He was telling them, Ready or not, here I come.

Getting Started

1. What games did you enjoy playing when you were a child?

2. What games do children enjoy playing today?

3. What "games" might some Christians be playing when Jesus returns for the church?

Searching the Scriptures

In 2 Corinthians 11 Paul defended his apostolic authority by reporting his pedigree and his trials. In the first part of chapter 12, Paul continued to defend his apostleship. First he claimed to have received divine revelations (v. 1). He wrote, "I knew a man in Christ above fourteen years ago, . . . such an one caught up to the third heaven" (v. 2). Verse 7 makes it clear that Paul was referring to himself as the man who had been caught up to the third heaven.

Paul was uncertain whether he had gone to the third heaven by body and soul/spirit or whether by only soul/spirit (vv. 2, 3). Nevertheless, this miraculous revelation authenticated his apostolic authority.

What did Paul mean by "the third heaven"? The first heaven is the atmosphere around the earth. The second heaven is space, where the stars are. The abode of God and the good angels is the third heaven. So Paul was saying he had been caught up to the highest heaven, to the throne of God, where he heard things too wonderful to repeat (v. 4).

4. What does it say about Paul's character that he used a third person pronoun ("he") to refer to his being caught up to the third heaven?

5. What internal struggle did Paul relate (vv. 5, 6)?

6. Why did God give Paul a "thorn in the flesh" (v. 7)?

7. a. How long did Paul keep his visions and revelations of the Lord a secret (v. 2)?

  b. What does Paul's long silence and accompanying humility about such a tremendous experience tell you about how well Paul's thorn in the flesh worked?

Obviously, a proud person offends God.

Paul's thorn in the flesh buffeted him (v. 7). The word "buffet" means "to throw blows as with a fist." The affliction troubled Paul severely but necessarily.

8. Why do you think Paul did not disclose the particulars about his "thorn in the flesh"?

9. Paul's thorn in the flesh was "the messenger of Satan" (v. 7). What did Satan want to accomplish in Paul's life through the thorn?

10. What does Satan want to accomplish in a believer's life through "thorns in the flesh"?

11. What does God want to accomplish in a believer's life through "thorns in the flesh"?

Paul prayed three times that God would remove his thorn (v. 8), but God had sent it there to keep Paul humble. God would not remove it.

Does this mean that God did not respond to Paul's prayer? No, God answered, but He answered in a way different from what Paul had hoped. God responded to Paul's prayers by giving him the grace to put up with the "thorn" (v. 9). God's grace supplied the power to make Paul strong despite his weakness (v. 10).

Do you have a thorn in the flesh? something painful? something that grates on your nerves? something that constantly irritates you? God has allowed it for a special reason. God wants to teach you through it and conform you to the image of His Son (Romans 8:28, 29).

If something irritates you and will not go away, you need God's grace to live godly in spite of it. God can help you; His "grace is sufficient" for you.

12. How has a "thorn in the flesh" helped you focus on eternal things and prepare for the coming day of reckoning before Christ your Judge?

13. How has God's grace been sufficient for you in your everyday life?

Paul continued to defend his apostolic authority by writing about his position and his performance. In 2 Corinthians 12:11 he referred to his position among the other apostles. He did not want to defend himself by talking about himself (as he was doing), but the Corinthians had compelled him to do so by not defending him before the impostors. He ranked well ahead of those so-called super apostles, who were in reality false apostles.

In verses 12 and 13 Paul wrote of his performance as a true apostle. Miracles authenticated the apostles' message. The book of Acts records some miracles performed by the apostles. Paul's life, too, exhibited miraculous works, thus showing that he was a true apostle.

Verses 14 and 15 show that Paul dealt with the Corinthians in love. Though they did not love him, he loved them dearly. Showing love is one of the best ways to deal with difficult people.

14. Read Romans 5:8. How does this verse help you love those who seem unworthy of your love?

Jesus taught that the second-greatest commandment is that we love our neighbors (Matthew 22:39). How can believers expect to fair well before Christ their Judge if they never learn to love their neighbors while on earth? Paul's love for the Corinthians not only endured, it increased even though their love for him waned. Certainly Christ will commend Paul for his deep love for unloving people.

Paul went out of his way to keep from offending the Corinthians (2 Corinthians 12:16–18). In fact his overarching goal was to see the Corinthians built up in the faith (v. 19). Paul wanted the Corinthians to grow, and he made every effort to help them along the way. Though Paul had heard a good report from Titus (7:4–9), he was leery that the revival in Corinth would be shallow and short-lived (12:20). This possibility caused Paul fear and concern.

While love for the Corinthians had always motivated Paul, he promised not to spare the unrepentant (v. 21). In essence, Paul was warning the Corinthians of his coming. Paul loved them too much to let them continue in disobedience. One day Christ will return to visit us. We, like the Corinthians, must be ready for that visit.

Paul promised to manifest the power of Christ when he went to Corinth (13:1–3). The Corinthians thought he was weak when he was present, but Paul promised he would deal sternly yet lovingly with the unrepentant minority.

15. How can a parent's disciplining a child indicate genuine love for the child?

Paul told the Corinthians to examine themselves (v. 5). Instead of spending all their time and energy trying to determine the genuineness of his apostleship, they should have been testing the genuineness of their own faith. They had been judging Paul. They should have been looking at the sinful things going on in their church instead, and they should have put them away.

16. What purpose does self-examination serve in the life of the believer? (See 1 Corinthians 11:28–31.)

Paul would have preferred to have the Corinthians deal with the problem of their sinful practices so he would not have to visit them with severity (2 Corinthians 13:10). He wanted them to manifest purity and perfection (v. 7) and to do right, not wrong.

Paul finished his letter with a brief conclusion, starting with, "Finally, brethren" (v. 11). In spite of all their troubles and problems and their attacks on his authority, Paul still called the Corinthians "brethren."

17. What four admonitions did Paul give the Corinthians in verse 11?

If the Corinthians would live in unity and peace with one another, the God of love and peace would dwell with them (v. 11). Their squabbles had, in effect, shut God out of their midst. God is a loving God and the giver of true peace. If they lived in harmony with one another, they would experience the full assurance of the love and peace of God in their hearts.

The benediction found in the last verse is the most comprehensive benediction found in Paul's epistles. In this benediction, he mentioned all three Persons of the Trinity. He prayed that the Corinthians would have the grace that flows from our Lord and Savior, the love that flows from the Father, and the communion, or fellowship, that derives from the Holy Spirit. This Trinitarian benediction appropriately concludes the book of 2 Corinthians.

Making It Personal

18. How can you guard your life against sinful pride?

19. What situation are you dealing with that requires a generous supply of divine grace?

20. Think through what you have learned in your study of 2 Corinthians. What applications did God lay on your heart?

Commit to God to follow through with those applications so Christ might find you serving Him when He returns.

21. Commit 2 Corinthians 12:9 to memory. Write the verse below.